WARREN HASTINGS

WARREN HASTINGS

WARREN HASTINGS

BY

SIR ALFRED LYALL

 BOOKS FOR LIBRARIES PRESS
FREEPORT, NEW YORK

First Published 1889
Reprinted 1970

INTERNATIONAL STANDARD BOOK NUMBER:
0-8369-5607-9

LIBRARY OF CONGRESS CATALOG CARD NUMBER:
73-140364

PRINTED IN THE UNITED STATES OF AMERICA

CONTENTS

CHAPTER I

WARREN HASTINGS was born at Daylesford, in Wor-
cestershire, in December, 1732. He was of good and
ancient stock; although Burke, the son of a country
solicitor, has described his origin as low, obscure, and
vulgar—an unfounded calumny ventilated, like many
others of the sort, by Sir Philip Francis. One of his
name certainly held the manor of Daylesford in the time
of Henry the Second; but the family suffered heavily in
the great civil war of the seventeenth century, when John
Hastings, then at Yelford Hastings in Oxfordshire, lost
the greater part of his lands and his money in the service
of Charles the First; and in 1715 Daylesford was sold
to a merchant of Gloucester by Warren Hastings' great-
grandfather. Subsequent generations must have been
pressing rather closely on each other, for Warren
Hastings himself was born only seventeen years later,
his father having married, without means, at the age of
fifteen. The poor mother died a few days after giving
birth to her second son; while the father married again,
took holy orders when he was old enough, and died
obscurely in the West Indies; having failed through
improvidence in most of life's affairs, though he succeeded
in accidentally producing a very remarkable son.

𝔈   B

Perhaps no man of undisputed genius ever inherited
less, in mind or money, from his parents, or owed
them fewer obligations of any kind. It is not possible
to find in Pynaston Hastings any trace of the character or intellectual qualities of his son; the mother
died in child-birth, while the father seems to have
abandoned him very soon afterwards; for in a petition
presented to the Lord Chancellor by their uncle in 1733,
on behalf of Warren Hastings and his sister Anne, it is
said that their father had withdrawn himself to some
distant place, leaving the children wholly unprovided
for. The boy was at first placed by the grandfather at
a charity school; but at the age of twelve he had the
good luck to be sent by his uncle, who had taken charge
of him, to Westminster. The system and mode of life
at the large public schools of England, with all their
grave deficiencies in regard to methodical teaching, have
been usually good for the development of character and
scholarship in boys of real intellectual ability. Their
innate tastes and aptitudes, which need only free play
and example, find room and stimulus, where the aver-
age schoolboy only discovers that loose discipline means
liberty to be idle. Hastings worked hard, was good on
the river, and was elected to a king's scholarship in the
year 1747, as the names engraved on the wall of his
dormitory still testify. But his uncle died, and he was
made over to the care of a distant connection, who
happened to be a director of the East India Company,
and who insisted, against the remonstrance of the Westminster head-master, that Hastings should give up his
high hopes of distinction at a university, and should
learn accounts from Mr. Smith of Christ's Hospital

before going out to Bengal as a writer on the Company's establishment. It was thus by a series of fortuitous events that, after entering the world in very unpromising circumstances, after being passed on from one kinsman to another, and after losing all his natural guardians, Warren Hastings came to be shipped for India in the year 1750, being then seventeen years old, about the same age as his father when the son was born.

All readers of Macaulay's famous *Essays* have some general knowledge of the political condition of India at the time when Warren Hastings landed in Calcutta, toward the end of 1750. The dynasty of the Mogul emperors, founded by Baber in the sixteenth century, was the longest and strongest that had ever ruled in the country. The great expanse of open and comparatively level country, which stretches from the Indus and the Himalayas south-eastward to the Ganges and the sea, had been completely under the imperial sway; the Deccan was a province of the empire, and its jurisdiction was recognised in almost all parts of the Indian continent, except the extreme south. The emperors exercised dominion, in fact, over an immense collection of districts, provinces, subordinate chiefships, and kingdoms; in most of which Mahommedans had settled, had converted great numbers of the population, and monopolised almost all the chief offices and commands. Under the descendants of Baber this dominion lasted in full vigour about one hundred and fifty years; but it was ill welded, heterogeneous, incoherent, and mainly held together by a foreign mercenary army and the constant influx of fresh blood from the original homes of the ruling race

beyond the Afghan mountains. Its strength and stability
were already much shaken when Aurungzebe's death, in
1710, closed a remarkable series of able monarchs; and
it slipped so rapidly out of the feeble hands of his
successors that in 1750 it was in a state of widespread
dilapidation. All the chief native principalities—with
whom, as the "country powers," we had so much fighting
and treaty-making during the remainder of the century—
were just then in the earlier stages of formation; their
founders were collecting armies, scrambling for lands,
and striking openly for separate independence; the
territory of the empire was being pulled to pieces like a
child's map. The sack of Delhi in 1740 by Nadir Shah
the Persian had ruined the capital and destroyed the
resources of the imperial government. Then followed
the invasions of Ahmed Shah, one of the captains of
Nadir Shah's host, and the founder of the present
dynasty of Afghan Amirs; who descended upon India
with a swarm of Durânis, broke down the defences of
the empire's north-western frontier, and seized all the
adjoining provinces. In the Central Punjab the Sikhs
were in full insurrection; the Mahrattas had broken
loose in the west, had subdued or devastated great tracts
of country, had overrun Central India, and were levying
tribute throughout the richest districts of the empire.
The death in 1748 of the great Nizam, who had made
himself virtually king of the Deccan, had thrown
Southern India into the confusion of the Carnatic war.
And even in the rich plain which extends from the
Himalayan mountains to the Bay of Bengal—the
country which has always been the seat of empires in
India and the source of their prosperity—the Delhi

emperors were fast losing all authority; they could
neither keep their troops in the field nor collect the
revenue.   An able and ambitious adventurer, usually
from Central Asia, obtained the appointment to a
governorship and proceeded to turn it into a family
possession ; or a bold military leader extorted from the
Mogul the nominal title of Viceroy, Commander-in-Chief,
or of some other great office under the crown, which
afforded him a pretext for levying troops and collecting
revenue on his own account.   In Rohilcund the Rohilla
chiefs, who were mostly Afghan soldiers of fortune, had
in this manner established themselves as nominal feuda-
tories of the empire, but in reality as independent
usurpers of the governing power, and of the crown lands
and revenue.   In Oude the Nawab Vizier (or Vicegerent)
was laying the foundations of an extensive sovereignty ;
while Bengal was ruled by Ali Verdi Khan, a saga-
cious and capable governor who kept on good terms
with the English traders at Calcutta, and whose chief
concern was to repel the incursions of the predatory
Mahrattas.

The course of events which first attracted English
commercial enterprise toward India, and latterly opened
the way to territorial acquisitions, belongs to and is
connected with the current of general history.   The
conquest of the eastern shores of the Mediterranean and
of the adjoining territories by barbarian invaders from
North-Eastern and Central Asia, interrupted the old
trade-routes overland to India by Syria and Bagdad,
and from the Black Sea down the Tigris into the Persian
Gulf.   At first the trade shifted to Egypt and the Red
Sea ; but when the Turkish Sultan, Selim, overran Syria

and seized Egypt in 1516, all the lines of commerce overland with Southern Asia were broken. This closing of the ancient trade routes diverted into new channels the adventurous mercantile spirit of Europe. The cities of the inland sea had lost their former advantage of position : Venice was cut off from her Asiatic communications ; and the career of mixed commerce and conquest was taken over by the ocean-going nations of the West. In America, England and France contended during one hundred years for territorial predominance by conquest and colonisation ; in India the struggle began with commercial competition. Toward the middle of the eighteenth century the colonial and commercial rivalry between the two nations had reached its climax all over the world ; and the naval superiority of England was gradually developing out of the contest. In the Indian peninsula the news of the peace of Aix-la-Chapelle (1748) had caused a formal cessation of hostilities between the French and English ; but in the same year began the war between the rival claimants for the rulership of the Carnatic province, in which the French and English trading companies took opposite sides, when the incomparable superiority of Dupleix and Bussy gave the victory at first to the French candidate.

Under the system, first invented by Dupleix, of acquiring a dominant influence in the political disputes of the native princes by maintaining a force drilled and armed on the European model, France had acquired in 1750 a decided ascendency. A kind of unofficial warfare went on for two or three years ; but the system of Dupleix, whose real genius has been somewhat overpraised, relied mainly upon complicated and very unscrupulous intrigues with the native competitors for rule in the Indian peninsula; a network in which he himself became ultimately entangled. The English were compelled, very reluctantly, to follow his example : they were forced to contract alliances and to join in the loose scuffling warfare that went on round them; and they soon proved themselves better players than the French at the round game of political hazard. There was great jealousy and disunion, as usual, among the French leaders in India : their ambitious designs alarmed their native friends; and latterly some unlucky enterprises of the French party, together with the discovery in France that these military operations were loading the Company with debt, induced the French Government to recall Dupleix, and to sign with the English in India a treaty renouncing on both sides all further interference with disputes between native States. The position thus abandoned was never regained by France; for when regular hostilities began again two years later, Lally was beaten after hard fighting in South India; and Clive's victory at Plassey (1757) opened out for the English a much longer and more important field of war and diplomacy in Bengal, where the French from that time forward had no footing.

The earliest years of Warren Hastings' residence in Bengal fell, therefore, within that period when the East India Company first began to interfere systematically in the quarrels of the country. The example of interference set by the French, the practice of following suit in India to the lead in Europe, and of extending to Asia any war that broke out between France and England at home; the perils of the tumultuous discord all round their frontiers, and the opportunities offered by such a state of affairs—all these risks and temptations were inevitably bringing the English in India at this time upon the political stage. Up to this epoch they had done their best, on principle, to avoid fighting, to abide by the sea-shore, and to keep clear of territorial responsibilities; but from 1757 commenced the era when conquest became allied to commerce, and when trade carried and followed the flag into the interior of India.

Hastings lived two years at Calcutta, working as assist-ant in the Secretary's office; he was transferred in 1753 to the factory at Kasimbazar, near Moorshedabad, on the Ganges, where his duties seem to have been connected with the silk spinning business, and in 1755 (or 56) he was promoted to the Factory Council. Factories were trading posts and warehouses established at some of the principal commercial towns, where goods sent out from Europe were sold, and Indian produce or manufactures collected for despatch home. Each of them seems to have been managed in early days by its own president and council; subordinate of course to the chief Presidencies at the seaports. Most of them were fortified and guarded by armed men, and within their limits the authority of the chief agents was practically unlimited. Within four months of Hastings' arrival at Kasimbazar occurred the death of Ali Verdi Khan, the old Nawab of Bengal, an event which at once changed the aspect of affairs in Bengal, because it laid open that province, one of the richest in India, to the rising flood of discord and mis-rule that was spreading all round. Ali Verdi Khan was one of the imperial viceroys who had made himself independent; his firm government had maintained a

barrier against external invasion, and had kept peace
within his borders; but the caprice and violence of his
grandson and successor, Suraj-u-Dowlah, produced a state
of terror, insecurity, and confusion. Incapable despotism
is shortlived anywhere, especially in Asia; and when
surrounded by disorganisation it has no chance at all.
The instinct of self-preservation at once finds its natural
remedy in conspiracy and revolt; the strongest elements
in society rise rapidly to the surface, and the best and
boldest men come to the front. In 1756 no one in
Bengal regarded the English trading company as a
political force, or supposed that Suraj-u-Dowlah's quarrel
with them would speedily lead to his defeat and death,
and to the reduction of his kingdom under their authority. His first attack on them was quite unprovoked.
The English, hearing that war with France was just
breaking out in Europe, began to fortify Calcutta. The
Nawab ordered them to stop the work; the English
were obliged to disobey, for he had not the power and
might not have had the will to protect them against
the French. But their refusal enraged the Nawab, who
at once surrounded the factory at Kasimbazar, plundered
it, imprisoned the Company's servants, Warren Hastings
among the rest, and marched on Calcutta with ten thousand men, disregarding repeated offers of submission to
all his demands. Then followed, in June, 1756, the
tragedy of the Black Hole, when one hundred and
forty-six English prisoners were crushed for a night into
a room about twenty feet long by fourteen in width,
with two small grated windows; of whom twenty-two
men and one woman survived till the morning. The
Calcutta factory was destroyed; all the English trading

stations in Bengal were broken up, and the main body of the Company's servants took refuge upon a little island in the river below Calcutta, where they encamped like a shipwrecked crew, awaiting rescue. They were relieved in December by the arrival of Admiral Watson's fleet bringing Colonel Clive and some troops, when the scene was again changed by the recovery of Calcutta and the taking of Hooghly, the Nawab's chief military post near Calcutta. Suraj-u-Dowlah, who had returned to Moorshedabad, reappeared with an army before Fort William, but after an indecisive night engagement he made peace with the English and restored their factories. In the East treaties mean little more than temporary truces ; the Nawab, naturally anxious to strengthen himself against formidable intruders within his own borders, began to negotiate with the French at Chaudernagore, and was obviously dangerous and untrustworthy ; so hostilities began in June, and were practically finished in a fortnight at Plassey. Suraj-u-Dowlah was first defeated and next murdered by his own officers ; the throne became vacant, and the country masterless ; whereupon there ensued the era of puppet Nawabs set up by the English, who tried to reserve political power without administrative responsibility, a *régime* which produced more scandalous abuses and oppressions than the worst of all purely native governments.

Warren Hastings had been released from detention at Moorshedabad on the security of Mr. Vynett, chief of a neighbouring Dutch factory, and had opened a correspondence with the English at Fulta, the island to which they had fled from Calcutta. Drake, the Calcutta governor, sent him a letter for the Nawab full

of humility and submission, asking for a supply of
provisions; but Hastings, who knew that the Nawab
had his own difficulties, preferred to wait until he could
be approached in a less suppliant tone; rightly judging
that nothing could be gained by falling on their knees
before Suraj-u-Dowlah.   Some secret letters between
the Fulta party and the powerful native bankers at
Moorshedabad, who feared and detested the Nawab,
also passed through the hands of Hastings, but the
only effect was to make it unsafe for him to remain at
Moorshedabad; so he escaped to Chunar, and thence
went down the river Ganges to join the Calcutta refugees
at Fulta.   Here he met the widow of Captain Campbell,
whom he afterwards married, and in 1758 he wrote to
a friend that he was very happy, and found every good
quality in his wife.   But the poor lady died in 1759
after bearing him two children, neither of whom survived childhood; and of this brief episode in his eventful
life only the bare facts remain, like the names and dates
on some obscure stone among the historic monuments of
a great church.

When the fleet arrived he returned to Calcutta, which
was recovered after a slight resistance.   He bore arms
as a volunteer with the troops under Clive's command,
in the fighting round Calcutta and the taking of Hooghly
fort; and he had some share in conducting an abortive
negotiation with the Nawab himself.   When Mir Jáfir
succeeded, after Suraj-u-Dowlah's defeat and death, to
the Nawabship, Hastings was sent up as assistant to Mr.
Scrafton, the Company's representative with the new
government at Moorshedabad, and afterwards was appointed to succeed him.   The somewhat complicated

nature of the Company's occupations and interests in that quarter rendered his duties proportionately multifarious. The English were already the dominant political power in Bengal, so that their agent at the court was surrounded by intrigues; while he seems to have retained his connection with the neighbouring factory, and to have been charged with the collection of revenue assigned by Mir Jáfir to the Company. He also discovered and remedied a flaw in the documents under which Mir Jáfir had granted to the Company their first considerable territorial acquisition—a service on which Mr. Gleig[1] lays much stress, though in those days treaties and title-deeds were hardly worth the trouble of verbal rectification, being usually construed by the changing light of circumstance. Some of his correspondence about this time with Clive, who was then his chief at Calcutta, is quoted by Mr. Gleig; the subjects are unimportant, but the style of the two writers, especially of Clive, which has a Cromwellian tone about it, is well marked. Hastings took some official umbrage at finding that Nuncomar, who was already figuring as an important agent of the English, had been sent up to collect revenue within his jurisdiction without formal notice to himself; and Clive replied briefly that no slight was intended.

The position in which Hastings found himself at the court of the Nawab Mir Jáfir must have been one of considerable difficulty, for the English soon made the discovery, very often made by them since, that the establishment of puppet princes, which at first seems an ingenious and convenient device for keeping power and dropping

[1] *Memoirs of Warren Hastings.*

responsibility, is an invention that almost invariably fails. To upset a hostile Eastern ruler and to set up a friendly one, are simple remedies for obvious incommodities; but the client prince is soon found to be entirely dependent on his patrons for support, and to have an awkward though natural propensity for saddling them with the blame for all his misfortunes, crimes, and blunders. Mir Jáfir, who owed his place to the Company, had been obliged to pay heavily for it in land and cash, while the exorbitant pretensions of the Company to trade privileges disorganised his revenue; and the whole province was distracted by foreign attacks and internal conspiracy. He was threatened by Mahratta inroads; and Shah Álam, the new emperor, who was a wandering fugitive at Benares when his father died, had entered Bengal with some troops to upset the Nawab's authority. Shah Álam defeated his troops, very nearly took Patna, ravaged Behar with the help of a band of Mahrattas, threw the province into complete disorder, and considerably damaged the financial resources of the Company, who had to find troops for expelling him, while the Nawab's wasted land revenue could not find the money to pay them. Mir Jáfir's own regiment mutinied; his eldest son was killed by a stroke of lightning; conspiracies were forming all round him; the English pressed him for more than he could pay, and he began to find his situation intolerable. He did his best to shake off or counterbalance the English predominance by making overtures to the emperor and to the Dutch; by making away with ill-wishers and suspicious characters, and offering large presents to the Company's agents. But his affairs were in a plight so desperate as to be beyond his capacity for retrieving them; and on the departure of Clive, whose head and hand alone kept the whole intricate machinery at work, he was speedily dethroned by Mr. Vansittart, who put up Mir Kásim Alli in his stead. Warren Hastings seems to have felt some sympathy with the unlucky Mir Jáfir until he caused two widows of Ali Verdi Khan to be barbarously executed; but in any case the English agent at Moorshedabad was obliged to follow and act upon the policy of his principals at Calcutta, and he probably saw that Mir Jáfir's administration must come to an end. Mir Kásim proved a worse bargain to the Company than Mir Jáfir; he found the treasury empty, the pay of his army in heavy arrears, and a large debt due as usual to his English backers, who had taken the opportunity of the change in Nawabs to tighten instead of relaxing their restrictions on his independence, and to increase the abuses of their private trade. There was, it must be confessed, almost as much miserable incapacity just then at Calcutta as at Moorshedabad, for the two Nawabs, Jáfir Alli and Mir Kásim, could hardly have been weaker administrators than the Presidents, Holwell and Vansittart, who succeeded Clive, particularly since from 1761 Vansittart was incessantly thwarted and overridden by a majority of his Council. Moreover, Clive, before leaving India, had sent home a public despatch rebuking the Honourable Company somewhat roughly for harsh and injudicious treatment of faithful servants, for unjust and unworthy language, for jobbery and favouritism. To which the London Board replied that they had taken into consideration the gross indignities and insults conveyed by their President's letter, and positively ordered the immediate dismissal of all those who had signed it. Clive, who was in England, cared little for the wrath of the Directors, but others were turned out, and Hastings was transferred to fill one of these vacancies.

His removal from the Patna agency was probably very unfortunate, for he had already shown judgment and moderation; while he was replaced by a man absolutely unfit to deal with a complex and dangerous juncture of affairs. Mr. Ellis soon brought the altercations with the Nawab so near to the brink of an open rupture that Hastings was despatched again to Patna early in 1762, with a mission to inquire into the causes of some violent disputes that had broken out between the native government and the English factories, and to look into certain rumours that the Nawab was corresponding with the Vizier of Oude. The reports which Hastings submitted betray no bias against the Nawab; he gives an impartial account of the misconduct on both sides; he appreciates the Nawab's difficulties, showing that the Nawab's discontent and the country's troubles were largely attributable to the high-handed rapacity of persons trading or plundering under the Company's flag or uniform. In a letter which he wrote to the Governor in 1762 he protested vigorously against the abuses that he found prevailing:

"I beg leave to lay before you a grievance which calls loudly for redress. I mean the oppressions committed under sanction of the English name, and through want of spirit in the nabob's subjects to oppose them. This evil, I am well assured, is not confined to our dependants alone, but is practised all over the country by people assuming the habits of our sepoys and calling themselves our gomastahs. As, on such occasions, the great power of the English intimidates the people from resistance, so, on the other hand, the indolence of the Bengalees, or the difficulty of gaining access to those who might do them justice, prevents our having knowledge of the oppressions, and encourages their continuance, to the great, though unmerited, scandal of our government."

In short, the English were too strong and the Bengalees were too weak; the Company had decreed to itself exemption from the authority of the native officials, and every one else naturally emulated this shining example. The enormous profit of the private trade, which claimed to pass duty free, demoralised the English trading community and all who belonged to it. "Nothing," wrote Hastings, "will ever reach the root of these evils till some certain boundary be fixed between the Nawab's authority and our own privilege;" and he made proposals for adjusting quarrels upon this basis. The Nawab's objections, he remarked, were not so much to the framing of proper regulations, as to the absence of any kind of authority to enforce their execution; but such an authority the majority in Council were not inclined to provide. After three months Hastings returned to Calcutta having accomplished nothing; and he went up again to Patna before the end of the year with Vansittart, who had determined to settle matters, which were growing worse and worse, in person. The English Company was privileged to carry on the shipping trade at the seaports free of customs; but their agents dishonestly pretended to exemption for their goods from all tolls and duties levied in the interior of Bengal, to the great damage of the inland revenue. Vansittart and Hastings settled with the Nawab a scheme for ending these malpractices and placing the whole inland trade upon an equal footing; but it was prematurely disclosed, and roused furious opposition from a majority of his Council, who condemned and cancelled the President's agreement, and passed resolutions upholding their factories in resistance to the Nawab's revenue officers. Hastings steadily supported the Governor in opposing these resolutions; and in one instance he voted against them alone, contending with all his strength for honest dealing and free trade. He said:

" As I have formerly lived among the country people in a very inferior station, and at a time when we were subject to the most slavish dependence on the government, and have met with the greatest indulgence, and even respect, from zemindars and officers of government, I can with the greater confidence deny the justice of this opinion ; and add further, from repeated experience, that if our people, instead of erecting themselves into lords and oppressors of the country, confine themselves to an honest and fair trade, they will be everywhere courted and respected."

The Nawab, greatly incensed, fell back at last on the expedient of abolishing all internal duties on trade, whereby he deprived the English of all the advantages of their unjust insistence on special exemption. The Calcutta Council denounced this act as treacherous and exceedingly damaging to them, and when Hastings who had been Vansittart's sole supporter in these debates objected to this denunciation as unreasonable, there followed high words with one Mr. Batson, who so grossly insulted Hastings that he sent him a challenge, though the duel was stopped.

With such politicians at Calcutta, and with such an agent at Patna as Mr. Ellis, who was irritable, headstrong, and incompetent, some collision was evidently

imminent. It came in 1763 when Mr. Ellis, hearing that
the Nawab was about to attack the English factory,
anticipated him by the bold stroke of seizing Patna city ;
but his troops were soon dispersed, and all the Englishmen were captured, to be massacred afterwards in cold
blood. The Company declared war against Mir Kásim,
and very soon drove him across the Ganges, whereupon
Mir Jáfir was reinstated in the Nawabship, which he
held in a feeble and fictitious manner until the next year,
when he died. Hastings, who was on the Council at
Calcutta, recorded in a minute his disapproval of these
proceedings ; stating that his purpose had been to resign
the service, since his unavailing protests had only kept
alive the disputes and dissensions round the Council
table ; but that as a dangerous and troublesome war had
now fulfilled his forebodings, he thought it his duty to
remain for the time. In 1764, however, Vansittart left
for England, and Hastings followed early in 1765, leaving
Bengal affairs in great disarray until Lord Clive returned
to set them in some order. In the meanwhile Shuja-u-
Dowlah, the Vizier of Oude, had advanced upon Patna
from the north, but had been defeated at Buxar by Major
Munro, who followed him across the Ganges into his
own territory and took Allahabad—an event of historical
importance, as it marks the first step beyond the north-
west frontier of Bengal and Behar into a wider and
thenceforward unlimited field of war and politics. The
Court of Directors foresaw the consequences of these extended operations and strenuously disapproved ; insisting
earnestly upon a strict adherence to the commercial
character and interests of the Company ; but the arrangements concluded were necessarily confirmed, and Lord

Clive's acceptance next year of the Dewanni virtually
established the English as a territorial power in India.

It must be allowed that Warren Hastings had passed
with credit and integrity through the most discreditable
and corrupt period in the annals of the East India Company.   In the midst of a general scramble for money he
never stooped to gains that were sordid or dishonest;
and at a time when most of the English were either
intoxicated by power or infuriated by misfortune—
demoralised by the cruelty and treachery which they saw
all round them—Hastings preserved, so far as can be
known from contemporary record, a character for equity
and moderation.   He engaged in private trade and contracts, as was the custom at that time of all the Company's servants whose chief emoluments came from that
recognised source.   But he had no turn for commerce,
which probably interested him less than politics; and
Raymond, the French translator of the *Sair Matákharin,*
says that he was obliged to borrow money from an
Armenian merchant for his expenses in going home.

For the period itself the only excuse to be made is
that it was very short, and so crowded with strange incidents, perilous adventures, and precipitate changes, that
one cannot wonder if the actors in such a drama lost their
heads.   In June 1756 the Company had been turned out of
Fort William and all their up-country factories in Bengal;
part of their establishment was in the Black Hole; the
rest, half-starved, upon an island in the Hooghly river.
Within twelve months the Company were virtually lords
of Bengal, and all the treasures of the State and resources
of the provinces were at their absolute disposal; the
French had lost all their settlements; their trade, up to

that time considerable, was annihilated, and the export business of the country had become an English monopoly. A few years later the Company found themselves *de facto* rulers of Behar, the great province that extends from Bengal proper westward up to the Ganges at Benares, four hundred miles from Calcutta. They had come for commerce and had found conquest; they had been compelled to choose between their own expulsion and the overthrow of the native government; they fought for their own hand, and won so easily that they found the whole power and responsibility of administration thrust upon them without warning, experience, or time for preparation.

A government that is upset at the first touch hardly imposes much respect or forbearance at the hands of adversaries who are restrained by no principles of public policy. A country that can be subdued by a mere band of some fifteen hundred foreigners, and reduced at once to a chaotic state of disorder and helplessness, so that it falls suddenly and completely into the hands of a set of trading adventurers uncontrolled by any regular authority or by the public opinion of their own people—such a prize is a terrible temptation to the morality of the victors. From 1760 to 1765, the interval between Clive's leaving and returning to Bengal, there was literally no effective control or governing authority in the provinces; and the evils of political anarchy were enormously enhanced by using the English flag as the standard and trade-mark of most unjust and injurious commercial privileges. At this time, and for many years afterwards, it was a principle with the East India Company to avoid and disown the assumption of any power that might imply territorial independence; they feared that it might involve them

with foreign nations in India, and that their sovereign
rights would be at once claimed by the Crown at home.
It was chiefly upon this ground that they pursued and
countenanced the disastrous method of putting up native
princes to reign nominally over countries where the
English were complete masters of all the springs of
authority and sources of revenue; nor is it surprising
that Lord Clive on his return found the settlement in a
deplorable situation—"a presidency divided, headstrong
and licentious, a government without nerves, a treasury
without money, and a service without subordination,
discipline, or public spirit."

It has been necessary to refer, though as briefly as possible, to the condition of Bengal when Warren Hastings
left it, in order that the general course and connexion
of the affairs of his time may be fairly understood; and
for the same reason some mention must be made of Lord
Clive's proceedings when he took up again the governorship of the Presidency in September, 1765. Lord
Clive came out armed with full powers to restore internal order, and to extricate the Company from external
complications. He laid down strict regulations for
checking commercial abuses and official corruption. He
made some attempts to improve the administration;
and he took one step of the highest importance, when he
accepted from the nominal Emperor of Delhi a grant of
the Dewanni of Bengal, Behar, and Orissa. The Dewan
under the empire had been the imperial commissioner for
the revenue and finance of a province, who was charged
with the duty of superintending and accounting for the
collection of revenue, defraying the expenses of the imperial troops within his circle, providing for the cost of

the civil establishments, and remitting the balance to headquarters. The acquisition of the Dewanni obtained for the Company its first formal status of recognised jurisdiction in India ; it gave a certain regularity to their proceedings and stability to their position. The English were henceforward something more than a formidable body of irresponsible foreigners interested only in private enterprise, although their nominal rank and functions in the State were still far from representing the real force of their actual interference with its machinery. Out of the revenues which they controlled they now maintained a standing disciplined army ; they held the sword as well as the purse ; foreign trade and foreign politics were both entirely in their hands ; they confirmed their own commercial privileges and they arranged external alliances ; the remaining attributes of sovereignty they were content to leave to the Nawab at Patna and his titular emperor somewhere in the vicinity of Delhi. We can easily understand why the Company persisted so long in these contrivances for securing the advantages and avoiding the obligations of political supremacy in Bengal. They had advanced so far that they could not go back or stand still ; and yet every step which they took toward the open ground of territorial rulership was upon an untried and dangerous road. There was no precedent for the development of a trading company into a governing power ; their position was liable to challenge at home and abroad. Nevertheless it was this period of inconsistencies and half measures, of divided authorities and clashing jurisdictions, that produced and prolonged all the complicated disorders and internal abuses which surrounded the earlier stages of Warren Hastings' subsequent governorship. We shall see, hereafter, that the first attempts of the Crown to interfere rather served to multiply than to mitigate the elements of administrative discord.

Hastings remained in England from 1765 to 1769, and of the manner in which he employed this time his biographers have found very few traces. His only son died just before his return, and although fourteen years' residence in India was usually sufficient in those days to provide any Englishman with ample means for living four years at home, it seems certain that Hastings took home very little money, and that his generous attempt to assist his relations even led him into some embarrassment. No one can deny that this undisputed fact is strong evidence as to early character, or that in this respect the whole career of Warren Hastings stands out in strong contrast against contemporary practice, in England not much less than in India; for the notion that office meant before all things emolument was still accepted with much indulgence everywhere, and was by no means extinct among place-hunters in England itself. He had not been twelve months at home before he applied to be again employed in India, and when the Court of Directors, for reasons not explained, declined his services, he took to literature and the reading of books. His acquaintance with Dr. Johnson, which Boswell mentions, shows that he had some access to the best literary society of the day; and if he had lived a century later his name would probably have been seen in some of the reviews or magazines. But the public of the eighteenth century was a small circle, interested in a range of subjects infinitely narrower than the wide and

varied list which now supplies every month fresh *menus*
of astonishing diversity, imported, like the fruit and the
flesh of our dinners, from all parts of the habitable
world. The special literary gift which brought success
to a writer of essays or verses at that period, and stamped
him as an author of taste or erudition, was not in
Hastings—the classic or academic style is a plant of hot-
house culture—nor indeed did his capabilities even lie
that way. His clear mind was at its best in the arrangement and statement of facts, and in plain, forcible
representation of a complex situation of affairs, with all
their causes and consequences distinctly indicated. When
he was either writing or speaking on such questions, his
style, like that of his great contemporary Lord Clive,
was as strong and full as it was mediocre and thin when
he was composing elegant verses or dissertations. His
evidence before the Committee of the House of Commons
in 1766 attracted the attention, according to Mr. Gleig,
of both the Court of Directors and the Ministry ; and
induced the Court to appoint him two years later to a
seat in the Presidency of Madras, as a gentleman who
had served them many years in Bengal with great ability
and unblemished character.

He sailed from Dover early in 1769, having been
obliged to borrow money for his outfit. It is well known
that during this voyage he became intimate with the
Baroness Imhoff, who was going out to Madras with
her husband, and whom Mr. Gleig describes as a gifted
young person between whom and her husband there was
no conformity at all, either of tastes or disposition. She
nursed Hastings through a serious illness on shipboard ;
she was a clever, fascinating woman, under thirty years of

age, not much attached to her husband, whose attachment
to her seems to have been of a loose and soluble kind, and
the result was that she and Hastings became very intimate.
Her maiden name was Anna Maria Apollonia Chapusettin.
They landed together at Madras, where they lived, it is
said, chiefly with Hastings at his house on The Mount, until
Imhoff, who began with a commission in the Company's
army but gave it up for miniature painting, went off to
Calcutta in 1770.   In 1771 he was followed thither by
his wife, and Hastings arrived to assume the governorship
of Bengal in 1772.   A letter written from Calcutta just
after his arrival says that his residence at Madras had
"greatly increased his former reserve," and describes
Mrs. Imhoff as "about twenty-six years old, has a good
person and has been very pretty, and wants only to be
a greater mistress of the English language to prove that
she has a great share of wit."[1]   In 1773 Imhoff went
home, never, so far as is known, to return; but the
divorce was delayed until 1777, so the marriage of
Hastings with Mrs. Imhoff did not take place until
August of that year.   These facts, which are quite plain
and speak for themselves, prove against Hastings a
breach of the moral and social law upon which every
one must pass his own judgment according to his estim-
ate of the gravity of such offences in the circumstances
of this particular case; nor will the verdict have been
much affected by the attempts which the biographers of
Hastings have made to address public opinion in mitiga-
tion of an austere sentence.   Mr. Gleig dwells on the
misery of ill-assorted union and on the fatal yielding
to instinctive attractions elsewhere, "which render the

[1] *Echoes from Old Calcutta*, 134.

cup of domestic existence more bitter than ever;" but
whether he thinks that Hastings should or should not
have done the thing he did, is a point which he leaves
ambiguous. He declares rather boldly that the breath
of censure never fell upon the good name of either party,
and both he and Captain Trotter [1] suggest that Imhoff
judiciously retired in time from an awkward but not yet
utterly false position; while Captain Trotter assures
us that the bargain between Imhoff and Hastings was
honourably fulfilled on both sides. On this matter it is
sufficient to observe that contemporary opinion was not
altogether so charitable. However this may be, for
historical purposes the important point is that this was
the only incident of Warren Hastings' life, at a time and
in a society by no means straitlaced, which throws any
reflection upon his relations with women; that against
the subsequent conduct of the second Mrs. Hastings no
one has ever said a word; [2] that she was in every respect
a good wife to him, and that the marriage seems to have
been one of perfect accord and lasting affection on both
sides.

Returning, as Mr. Gleig phrases it, to "the more dry
details" of Hastings' official business at Madras, we find
very little worth record of his life, private or public,
during the two years of his residence there as member
of Council. He mentions in a letter to Sir George

[1] *Warren Hastings;* by Captain L. J. Trotter (1878).

[2] Even Francis, who liked gossip and local calumny, writes to
his wife : "The lady herself is really an accomplished woman ; she
behaves with perfect propriety in her new station, and deserves
every mark of respect." But Lady Impey and other leaders of
Calcutta society looked very coldly on her until she married
Hastings.

Colebrooke that the abilities of the President (Mr. Du
Pré) left him little room for exertion beyond the limits
of his own particular department, the export warehouse ;
an important branch of the commercial business which
Hastings thoroughly reorganised with profit to his
employers and credit to himself. Nevertheless it is
remarkable that he should have played so subordinate
a part in the political transactions connected with his
tenure of office, which were complicated, considerable,
and ill managed by the Madras Council. Three rival
powers, Hyder Ali of Mysore, the Nizam of Hyderabad,
and the Mahrattas, were at that moment contending for
supremacy in the Indian peninsula, and each of them
alternately threatened the Company's possessions, or
proposed an alliance against the others. The Directors
in London incessantly enjoined upon the Madras government the necessity of avoiding alliances which were no
better than intrigues, and military operations which
exhausted in war the funds that were meant for trade.
The true policy, they said, was to stand aloof and let
the country powers weaken themselves by constant
fighting, whereas " the power which you help to beat the
rest will certainly turn its arms against us whenever
it is strong enough, and your allies will be constantly
negotiating a secret understanding with your enemies."
There can be no doubt that events justified the predic-
tions and warnings of the Directors, who at this time
laid earnest and incessant injunctions upon their Indian
governors to abstain from all extensions of territory and
from intermeddling in the quarrels of the " country
powers." But the Council at Madras thought a policy
of isolation unsafe when they were surrounded by

dangerous neighbours, and preferred to take a hand in
the game of politics, with the result that after much
unsuccessful and expensive fighting, and after some
instructive experiences of the value of treaties with
feeble and faithless allies, they concluded a peace which
left Hyder Ali deeply offended, and the Mahrattas more
than ever masters of the situation. From his correspondence with some of the Directors, Warren Hastings
appears to have defended the proceedings of his Council
on the ground that they acted for the best in very
dangerous circumstances; for the Madras Presidency
was threatened by Hyder Ali and the Mahrattas, had
been deserted by the Nizam, and was greatly alarmed by
rumours of a French war. But subsequent events went
far to prove that the perils and misfortunes which beset
Madras a few years later were distinctly attributable to the
mistaken policy of contracting engagements with Hyder
Ali and the Mahrattas, which could not be fulfilled without offending one or the other power. When Hyder
Ali had been utterly defeated by the Mahrattas in 1771
he applied for help to the English, who refused, and
thereby incurred the resentment of their most dangerous
neighbour in the peninsula. Ten years later he took
his revenge; and it will be seen that the storm which
then burst a few years later upon Madras, and very
nearly overwhelmed that Presidency, was also one of the
main causes why Hastings, then Governor-General, was
driven into narrow straits and rather desperate political
navigation.

CHAPTER II

THE GOVERNORSHIP OF BENGAL (1772-74)

THE Indian career of Warren Hastings is divided into two periods of almost equal length but of very different character. During his first residence of fourteen years in the country he served with credit in subordinate offices; but he does not seem to have carried home with him any reputation for signal ability or remarkable promise. In the second period of nearly thirteen years, dating from his assumption of the Bengal Governorship in 1772, his fortune was very different. After two years' work at Madras he was promoted to be President and Governor of Bengal, an appointment which he probably owed chiefly to the ability which he had shown in reforming the Company's commercial administration at Madras; for affairs at Calcutta were in a condition that required to be set right by some one who possessed the rare quality of tried integrity and personal incorruptibility. This position, which was greatly enlarged two years later by transformation into the Governor-Generalship, Hastings retained for thirteen years. No subsequent Governor-General has held anything like so long a tenancy of the office; nor has any of his successors had such difficulties to surmount with means so small and responsibilities so great, or to confront, with so little support, such powerful and vexatious opposition in India and England. His name is writ large across a very important page of Indian history ; and the period of his Governor-Generalship includes transactions of great complexity and consequence, which have been more talked about and less understood than any portion of the obscure and unattractive annals of our early administration in India. Most of the political complications in which he became entangled are sufficiently accounted for by the extraordinary confusion that prevailed all over India at this time ; and we have also to remember that the same period was one of violent jarring collision among parties at home, of misrule by incompetent Ministers, and of national discredit and misfortune ; of the American War, of Lord North's ministry, of ignominious failures and great moral depression among the English people.

Of the state of Bengal and Upper India when Warren Hastings took up the governorship in 1772 it is necessary to attempt some description ; though the method of interspersing short sketches of Indian history at intervals of this biography, with the vain hope of keeping the general reader at the true point of view, may very possibly neither interest nor instruct him. The dislocation of the empire was now so complete that it had been broken up into a number of independent principalities of varying extent and fighting strength. The possessions of the English in Bengal and Behar were surrounded on the land side by territories held under title-deeds and by tenures that were of no earlier date, and in no respect better, than their own, and by rulers whose dominion rested on a much less solid basis of military and financial

organisation. It was this state of affairs that gave the
English their opportunity of fixing themselves securely on
the coast, and that rapidly drew them on into the heart
of India. The country had been drained of specie by the
predatory invasions of the Persians, the Afghans, the
Mahrattas, and the Sikhs; trade and cultivation had
fallen very low; the chiefs and tribal leaders who were
contending for the land had no regular resources; they
had neither certain revenue nor standing armies; they
subsisted by the plunder of their marauding bands, and
were deserted by their troops on a defeat or upset by a
revolt. They were fatally jealous and suspicious of each
other, and they soon discovered that the English were
the only stable, solvent, disciplined, and trustworthy
power in the country. Beyond the northern border of
Behar lay, in 1770, a connected group of these chiefships, all under Mahommedan adventurers of foreign
origin, who had been lucky enough to seize certain districts, and were strong enough to levy from them
sufficient revenue for the support of their mercenary
troops, but whose position was rendered precarious by
the constant and imminent danger of attack by the
Hindu powers, the Sikhs, Mahrattas, and Jáths, who were
vigorous and popular representatives of the foremost
fighting tribes among the real natives of India, and who
were supported by religious enthusiasm and antipathy
to foreign domination. Of the Hindu powers, by far
the most formidable for attack were the Mahrattas;
although it may be observed that the occupation of the
Punjab by the Sikhs, who were practically hostile to
Islam, had cut the roots of the revival of any considerable Mahommedan rulership in Upper India by inter-

cepting the communication with Afghanistan and Central
Asia. No Mahommedan dynasty has ever flourished in
the north which did not constantly recruit its vigour by
fresh importations from beyond the Indus; and the
class of rulers represented by the Vizier of Oude, the
descendant by two or three degrees from an Afghan or
Persian, with a mixed army of indigenous mercenaries,
has always been ephemeral and has rapidly degenerated.

It was the policy of the English, when Warren Hastings
took charge of the Bengal Presidency, to maintain and
strengthen this group of Mahommedan chiefships along
their northern border as a barrier against invasion
from beyond, and especially against the depredations of
the restless, treacherous, and far-roving Mahratta hordes.
The most considerable among these potentates, whose
possessions, by their extent and situation, could best
serve our purposes, was undoubtedly the Vizier of Oude;
and the only effectual method of strengthening him was
by lending him disciplined troops to be stationed in his
country, and to be paid from his revenues, under treaty
engagements for mutual defence. The English were at
this time, and up to the end of Warren Hastings'
Governor-Generalship, honestly anxious not to extend
their territories, although they were quite aware that it
would be easy to do so. They saw quite clearly that by
accepting the Dewanni they had stepped forward across
the line which formally separated private enterprise from
public administration, and that they had reached the
point "which, to pass, would be an open avowal of
sovereignty." That the moment was particularly favourable for the assumption and extension of sovereignty
was no secret to the leading men who at that time

surveyed the situation in India. By the end of the Seven Years' War the French had been fairly beaten out of India; and in fact since 1763 no European rival has seriously interfered with us on Indian soil. It is a remarkable coincidence that the chronic invasions of India from Central Asia, which had for several centuries caused so many dynastic revolutions in the north, ceased at the same epoch, for the Afghan king, Ahmed Shah, retired finally behind the Indus in 1763; so that from that date we may reckon the commencement of an era during which the frontiers of India, by land and sea, were closed to all foreign powers except England. And we can now perceive plainly enough that so soon as the gates of India had been shut in the faces of all other maritime nations, our exclusive right of entry upon a vast arena, occupied only by a number of loose disorderly rulerships, offered great and tempting facilities to the unlimited expansion of our dominion. The course, indeed, that events have followed was actually foreseen a century ago; for it is a mistake to treat the growth of the British empire in the East as an equally marvellous and fortuitous run of national luck, of which the end would have amazed those who saw the beginning. There is ample evidence that the probability of the acquisition of all India by some European power was clearly discerned by competent observers who stood on the threshold of the period, stretching over a hundred years from the battle of Plassey to the great mutiny in 1857, during which all those strides of conquest were made which have carried us from the seaboard to the Himalayas and the Afghan frontier. To quote only one well-known instance, Lord Clive foresaw in 1765, and plainly warned the East India Company in a letter that has been often quoted, that they were already on the straight road to universal dominion in the country.

Upon that road, however, the Company were in no haste to set out. We find them strenuously declaring in 1768 that they are "determined to make the provinces of Behar, Bengal, and Orissa the utmost limits of our views or possessions on that side of India," a prudent and pacific resolution that was indeed very tolerably observed in Northern India, where we had no wars and made no material acquisitions until the end of the eighteenth century; and long before that date the real power of directing political affairs had passed from the Company to the Crown. The policy of the Bengal government, when Warren Hastings took charge of it, was, as we have said, to strengthen and give armed support to the Vizier of Oude, in order to build up a firm breakwater against the incessant fluctuations of predatory warfare that distracted Northern India. In 1771 and 1772 the incursions of the Mahrattas had struck terror and despondence into the hearts of the weak Mahommedan rulers whose possessions formed the outer barrier of our own provinces. Ten years earlier, in 1761, they had found a leader of military genius in Ahmed Shah the Abdallee, when by uniting their forces under his command they had driven the Mahrattas out of North India by his crowning victory at Paniput. But the Mahrattas had now returned; the Delhi emperor had placed himself in their hands; they had attacked the Rohillas, and had threatened Oude; the peace and protection of our own frontier could only be provided for by concerting measures of common defence with our neighbours. These were the grounds upon which the Bengal government had adopted the plan of establishing and consolidating along the eastern bank of the Ganges river, from Benares up to the Himalayas, a strong and friendly state under the Company's influence ; and it was in the prosecution of this design, as we shall see later, that Hastings sent troops to assist the Oude Vizier in subduing Rohilcund. This policy was at any rate successful ; for it gave Bengal a quiet and comparatively stable frontier for nearly forty years, and thus enabled our governors to make head against the serious embarrassments that encompassed our southern possessions in the Indian peninsula.

The internal condition of Bengal and Behar, at the time when Warren Hastings assumed charge of the Presidency at Calcutta, was exceedingly bad. There was no real government in the district, for all power was concentrated in the hands of the Company's representatives, who received the revenue and maintained their own troops ; so that the nominal administration of the Nawab became a mere fiction, impotent to repress crime or enforce justice ; every kind of fraud upon the revenue and extortion was practised by a crowd of native agents who pretended to act under the English name and authority ; while the contrast between the inordinate profits to be made in trade monopolies and the trifling salaries paid by the Company, had demoralised the whole English service. As a native pithily observed to Warren Hastings a year or two later, the trade of the country was ruined because the government of the country was concerned in it ; a heavy drain of specie for the foreign payments of the Company had hampered all transactions ; and in 1771 a wasting famine had visited Bengal. The

principal officers at Calcutta represented these evils to
the Directors at home; but the only true remedy lay in
the open assumption of the government by those who
held the power, which involved an entire change in the
form and character of the Company's constitution. It
is to be remembered that at this time the right of the
Company to possess territory had been very seriously
questioned in England, that their finances were seriously
embarrassed, and that in 1769 the Ministers only permitted them provisionally to retain for five years what
had been acquired, upon payment of a heavy bonus to
the Exchequer. It was in these unfavourable circumstances that Hastings took charge of the governorship,
armed with strict injunctions from the Company to redress abuses, to bring offenders to condign punishment,
to preserve peace abroad and to reduce expenditure at
home, but vested with no authority beyond that which
the charter of a trading settlement conferred on its chief
officer. The country was without a sovereign; there
was no power that accepted the duty of making laws
and enforcing them. The Company had indeed made
up their minds at last, in 1771, to "stand forth as
Dewan," that is, to appear as controllers and administrators of the revenue; but all the work of keeping down
crime and punishing it was still committed to the native
officials, who had lost all power and independence.

There is no fault to be found with the language in
which the Directors expressed their indignation at the
reports that had reached them of oppression, dishonesty,
and misrule in the provinces. They laid their secret
instructions on Hastings to make private investigation
into the conduct of his own colleagues and subordinates,

a sure way of setting them against him; they committed to his sole care the detection of crimes charged on the Company's servants; and they ordered him immediately to dismiss and prosecute the two chief native revenue officers. They had officially assumed administration of the finances of the country, and they pressed for closer superintendence of the judicial courts; though they still held back from dropping the cloak by setting aside the titular jurisdiction of the Nawab, and from openly undertaking the responsibility of regular government in all its branches. Hastings himself seems to have thought the fiction not worth maintaining. He perceived clearly enough that no solid improvement would be made, except upon the plain foundation of the assumption of the country's government by the English, and he shaped all his measures for gradually approaching that end; but in the meantime his methods of command were necessarily irregular, unauthorised, and indirect. He carried through nevertheless a fresh assessment of the land revenue, a matter of the highest importance; he formed plans for reforming and superintending the courts of justice, and for inspection of the public offices; he took up also the question of dealing effectively with the gangs of professional robbers who infested the frontier districts.

It must be mentioned that the chief of the revenue department, Mahomed Reza Khan, had been suspended upon the charge of heavy embezzlements; and that Nuncomar, afterward so notorious, had been selected on account of his well-known malignity towards the accused officer to collect evidence for the prosecution. The first suggestion of employing Nuncomar in this business had

come to Hastings in a secret despatch from the Court of
Directors ; and Hastings acted on it though he knew
the man to be dangerous, for in 1762 he had arrested
and confined him on suspicion of treasonable machina-
tions. Nuncomar's son was also simultaneously nominated manager of the household of the titular Nawab,
who, as a minor, was placed under the guardianship of
Muni Begum, widow of a former Nawab, a lady whose
seal or signature was freely used afterwards, with or
without her privity, in the documents fabricated by
Nuncomar for Hastings' discomfiture.

In writing to a friend upon these transactions Hastings said : "I expect to be much abused for my choice
of the Dewan (manager), because his father stands
convicted of treason against the Company . . . and
I helped to convict him. The man never was a
favourite of mine, and was engaged in doing me many
ill offices for seven years together." He also wrote
to the Directors in 1772 that he had taken care to
invest Nuncomar himself with no trust or authority,
and that no danger could come from the son, whose
disposition, unlike the father's, was placid, gentle, and
without disguise. Thus the son's office gave cover to
the father's power, and his simplicity to the father's cun-
ning, a situation so exactly suited to Nuncomar's special
aptitude for wire-pulling and surreptitious intrigues, that
it is hard to understand how Hastings could have been
induced to adopt tactics that were neither clever nor particularly creditable. In fact the Governor-General gained
nothing from them but the lesson that is invariably learnt
by Englishmen when they attempt to finesse against
Asiatics, for Mahomed Reza was finally acquitted ; and

Hastings conceived a deep distrust of Nuncomar, who had displayed a talent for preparing cases against, and laying snares for, an enemy, that seems to have startled Hastings with a curious presentiment of personal disquietude. The dislike and distrust was of long standing, since before he left Bengal in 1764 Hastings had received strong indications of Nuncomar's ill-will; and long afterwards, when he was indignantly repelling the charge of having murdered him, he wrote to a friend that he "was never the personal enemy of any man but Nuncomar, whom from my soul I detested even when I was compelled to countenance him." [1]

Meanwhile the Mahrattas had reinstated the Emperor Shah Álam in his palace at Delhi, and he had been compelled in return to join their expedition against the Rohillas, who were a kind of loose federation of Afghan chiefs holding possession of the rich tract that runs along the base of the Himalayas, from the Ganges eastward, up to the confines of Oude. About twenty years earlier the Mahrattas had extorted from these Rohillas, in the emperor's name, bonds for the payment of a quit-rent on their lands; and to these claims was now added another kind of score against them, dating from the victory of Paniput, when the Rohilla cavalry had been in the foremost line of the grand onset which routed the Mahrattas with vast slaughter. But for that very reason the emperor's policy in joining them was plainly ruinous to his own cause, since the only chance of his dynasty's revival lay in some kind of combination among the Mahommedans against their common enemy. And so it turned out, for the Mahrattas, after seizing a

[1] Gleig, iii. 357.

part of the Rohilla country and exacting heavy money
payment, speedily stripped the emperor himself of all
authority, and prepared for a fresh attack upon the
Rohilla chiefs, who implored aid from the Oude Vizier,
who in his turn asked the English to help him with
troops. If the Mahrattas were allowed to establish themselves in Rohilcund, it was certain that they would next
enter the lands of Oude, which lay just beyond; and
this would open out to them a road into the Company's
possessions, which were covered by the Vizier's territory,
and depended for their security upon his power of resistance. So the Rohillas made a defensive alliance with
Oude, covenanting to pay forty lakhs as the price of his
joining them to expel the Mahrattas; the English sent a
force to act with the Vizier and the Rohillas, and the
united army encamped on the Ganges in front of the
Mahrattas, who after some plundering forays drew back
westward into their own districts.

Such, therefore, was the general state and complexion
of affairs at the end of Hastings' first year of office, in
the beginning of 1773; and it may be said that no
English governor had ever found himself in a more
difficult position. When an Asiatic province or kingdom
comes under civilised dominion, it may be treated in one
of two ways,—either by pulling down the indigenous
system and rebuilding the administration on a European
plan, with any serviceable native material that can be
found in the country—or by allowing the old government to stand and continue exercising authority after its
own fashion, with certain limitations of its sovereignty.
But in Bengal, as has been seen, the native government
was left standing after it had lost all power; a mere

ruin that cumbered the ground, like a house in Chancery
which no one can repair because the title is unsettled.
The people had been extenuated by famine ; the treasury
was nearly empty; the official services, English and
native, were thoroughly discouraged; the moral and
material disorder was at its height.

Beyond his frontier Hastings saw the flood of Mahratta
invasion pressing higher and higher against the unstable
breakwaters of Oude and Rohilcund. In England the
Company were deep in debt, were contending for their
existence with the Ministers, and were acquiring an ill
reputation with the nation at large, among whom it
was then a new thing to hear of merchants taking and
governing Asiatic provinces, and to see their countrymen
returning from the East enriched by tribute or trade
monopolies, with money that had an Oriental odour of
violence and corruption. The appointment of Hastings
came just when public attention and indignation had
been seriously roused at home, when the Company's
credit at home and in India was at its lowest, when
money was most needed and least available for internal
reforms and external defence in Bengal. The moment
had come, so dangerous for weak and bad governments,
when improvements were imperatively demanded, and
Hastings was literally at his wits' end for ways and means.
It is necessary to take into account these circumstances
in passing judgment upon his foreign policy in 1772 and
1773, for while none of the transactions upon which he
has been arraigned have been so justly censured as his
share in the destruction of the Rohillas, it is certain that
he was in great embarrassment, that he was pressed upon
and surrounded by manifold difficulties, and that in his

time very few European statesmen would have long
balanced moral scruples against strong expedients for
meeting a political emergency.

The districts of Allahabad and Corah, which flanked
the Company's possessions on the north-west, had been
made over by Lord Clive in 1765 to the landless
and homeless Shah Álam in support of his imperial
dignity, and in order that they might not be occupied
by troublesome neighbours; but in 1771 the Mahrattas
had compelled the emperor to make over to them these
districts by a formal grant. This conveyance the Company determined to resist, so they placed the districts,
which were close to their own border, under their own
protectorate, and occupied Allahabad with a garrison.
To allow the Mahrattas entry into this part of the country
would have been to permit exactly what the original
arrangement with Shah Álam was intended to prevent,
the establishment of a predatory power that subsisted
upon conquest and ravages, in a position that threatened
equally the possessions of the Company and their ally
the Oude Vizier. The policy of the Company was to
consolidate the Vizier's territory, to separate him from
the Mahrattas, and to give him a substantial interest in
a defensive alliance against them. Accordingly, when
Hastings met the Vizier in September 1773 at Benares,
a treaty was concluded transferring the Allahabad
districts to the Vizier for a large sum of money, and for
a subsidy to be paid to the Company's troops that were
to co-operate with him in maintaining his possession.
The Vizier took the opportunity of sounding Hastings
on his project of expelling altogether the Rohilla chiefs,
and annexing to his own dominions all the country east-

ward of the Ganges, which would thus give him a
strong and continuous frontier line along that river.
He complained of the perfidy of the Rohillas as shown
by their double dealings with him and the Mahrattas, of
their failure to pay him the forty lakhs of rupees stipulated by an agreement of the previous year, and of the
danger to Oude from a possible combination between
the Rohillas and the Mahrattas against him. Hastings
made no objection to the proposal of a joint expedition,
saying only that the Vizier must find the money, as the
direct benefit would be his ; but toward the close of the
interview the Vizier drew back, alleging that the engagement was too weighty for him. Hastings readily agreed
to say no more about it, though he apparently still entertained the proposal as a kind of secret arrangement to
come into operation at a convenient time ; and the Vizier
wrote again in November proposing the joint expedition,
offering forty lakhs in cash with payment of the English
military expenses, and requiring the troops to be furnished
according to the Benares treaty. The reply, drafted by
Hastings, was to the effect that a brigade should be sent
to join the Vizier whenever he should require it for the
entire reduction of the Rohilla country, and this letter,
after having been laid before Council with an explanatory
minute, was, after formal consideration, approved and
despatched. In this minute the case was discussed
entirely on grounds of political expediency ; it was
argued that the Rohillas formed a weak and untrustworthy garrison of a very important point in the outer
line of defence against the Mahrattas ; that they were
capable of joining the Mahrattas against the Vizier, and
that the acquisition of their country by the Vizier would

considerably increase his wealth and security, in both of which advantages the Company would partake. On the other hand Hastings saw, and said plainly, that the expedition would be sharply criticised in England, and that "an unusual degree of responsibility was annexed to such an undertaking."[1]

No political act of Hastings has been more severely condemned than his share in the Rohilla war. Parliamentary orators have thundered against the sale and extirpation of a whole nation, as if a conqueror had depopulated Rohilcund, slaying and expelling all the inhabitants, or driving them like the ten tribes of Israel into exile and captivity, and utterly annihilating an able and admirable dynasty. Macaulay has contrasted "the golden days when the Afghan princes ruled in the vale of Rohilcund" with the unjust and cold-blooded bargain for their ruin and spoliation; and Mill, who dissimulates strong prejudice under a tone of judicial impartiality, has passed a stern sentence upon the whole transaction. The business, in short, has been so curiously misrepresented, that it is necessary here to give a short account of the origin and nature of the Rohilla domination in the province to which their name has become attached.

The word Rohilla, or mountaineer, seems to have been indiscriminately applied in India to the Afghans who during the seventeenth and eighteenth centuries came down in bands from their highlands to offer their services to the Delhi emperors. Dáud Khan and Rehmat Khan, the sons of one of these soldiers of fortune, entered the imperial army early in the eighteenth century, and

[1] Appendix 23. 5th Report.

obtained a grant of land in the province of Katehur, afterwards called Rohilcund. The son of Dáud Khan, Ali Mahmud, said by native historians to have been an adopted Hindu boy, raised himself to rank and consequence by seizing more land, enlisting Afghan retainers, procuring warrants of dignity and office from the court, and lastly by defeating a body of troops sent against him from Delhi, and killing the imperial commandant. This exploit so enhanced his reputation that all the roving blades and mercenary fighting men of the country side joined his company; he was able to bribe powerful officials at court, to enlarge his estates at his neighbours' expense, to amass rich booty by lucky expeditions, and after this time-honoured fashion to settle himself down into something like independent rulership over the greater part of Rohilcund. But in one of his continual broils and snatchings at contiguous property he unhappily fell into collision with the much more powerful founder of the Oude kingdom, Sefdar Jung, who was carrying on the same business on a larger scale, and who was also Vizier of the empire. The shark very nearly swallowed the pike; for Ali Mahmud was beaten, deserted by his banditti, surrendered, and was sent on parole to Delhi; his satrapy was broken up; and Rohilcund might never have existed at all if Ahmed Shah's descent upon India from Afghanistan had not drawn northward the armies and great officers of the empire. Ali Mahmud escaped back to his country, raised fresh levies, recovered his estates and authority, crushed out the resistance of the Hindu landholders; and in 1746 he was again in a position to extract from the demoralised ministry at Delhi his investiture with

the government of the whole province. At his death
in 1749 he left an independent chiefship to his six sons,
whom he committed to the care of two kinsmen; one
of whom, their uncle Rehmat Khan, thereafter termed
Háfiz, or guardian, showed much ability in consolidating, administering, and defending the dominion. The
Rohillas were again threatened by their old enemy
Sefdar Jung of Oude, but he was again recalled to
Delhi by news of danger to the capital; the Mahrattas
who had accompanied him were bought off by bonds,
and the Rohilla leaders now found leisure to set aside
the sons of Ali Mahmud, and to make a partition of the
territory among themselves. They fought well against
the Mahrattas on the field of Paniput; and as the house
of Timur was now virtually extinct at Delhi, the Rohilla
sirdars had by this time made out for themselves a
good working title and tenure, neither better nor worse
than those of other military adventurers who had
successfully followed immemorial usage in helping themselves to a kingdom in India. The towns were mainly
peopled by Hindus: the lands were cultivated, then
as now, by Hindu peasants; and large tracts were still
held by Hindu clans, who had for centuries paid to a
Mahommedan governor just as much revenue as he could
extract from them, and who cared little whether he
sent a part of their money to Delhi, or found his own
strong box a safer and more convenient treasury.

But the Mahrattas were pushing up north-eastward;
the Rohilla possessions lay open to their inroads, and Háfiz
Rehmat Khan, the captain of the Rohilla confederacy,
was not strong enough to keep them out, so he applied
for aid to Oude and to the English. In 1772 he made

with the Oude Vizier, Shuja-u-Dowlah, a treaty which was
promoted by the English general, Sir Robert Baker, and
signed in his presence, whereby the Vizier agreed, upon
payment of forty lakhs, to join Rehmat Khan against
the Mahrattas, who had actually passed the Rohilla
frontier. The Oude forces accompanied by an English
brigade accordingly made a junction with the Rohillas,
whereupon the Mahrattas hastily retired. The Vizier
demanded his money, but Rehmat Khan found difficulty
in raising it among his brother chiefs, put him off with
dilatory pleas, and finally it was not paid at all. To
Shuja-u-Dowlah, who lived in perpetual terror of a
combination between the Rohillas and Mahrattas against
himself, this failure to pay was probably not unwelcome :
he wrote to Hastings that he had been deceived, that
the treaty witnessed by an English general had been
broken, and he offered to pay the forty lakhs to the
English if they would assist him to root out the Rohilla
dominion, so that he might take possession of their
country. To this, as we have seen, the Governor-General
in Council finally agreed.

The Council seem at first to have hoped that the
Vizier would let the business stand over, and would not
call on them to fulfil their promise of sending troops.
But he lost no time in making his requisition ; the combined forces entered Rohilcund in the spring of 1774 ;
the Rohilla army commanded by Háfiz Rehmat Khan
met them, fought bravely, and was utterly defeated with
the loss of their chief in a single engagement. The
Vizier seized all the public treasure; his troops plundered
in the usual style ; the British commander was alternately
indignant at their cowardice in the field, at their excesses

after the battle, and at the Vizier's refusal to allow his
men a share of the prize-money; and the Council at
Calcutta dunned the Vizier for the forty lakhs due on
their agreement.

The Council believed the expedition to have been not
only a political success and a military exploit—they also
regarded it as a sound financial operation.   They wrote
home in October, 1774, that they had secured an advan-
tageous peace, and seventy lakhs of rupees; but Hastings
soon discovered, what he ought certainly to have foreseen, that by going into partnership with an Oriental
potentate, without taking a share in the direction as well
as in the profits of the enterprise, he had become responsible for the rapacity and inhumanity of successful Asiatic
warfare, at a distance which placed the Vizier far beyond
effective control from Calcutta.   It is extraordinary that
his Indian experience did not forewarn him of this contingency; and it must be admitted that he appears to
have been singularly blind to the political immorality of
the whole transaction, although its expediency, judged
simply as a move on the chess-board, is sufficiently defensible.   It is true that his barrier-policy may be said
to have been so far successful that the Vizier retained
undisturbed possession of his acquisitions until the end
of the century, when Rohilcund was ceded to the English.
Nevertheless nothing but the urgent necessity of self-
preservation can warrant unprovoked invasion of a
neighbour's country; and it must be confessed that the
war has left a stain upon the reputation of the Company
in India, where a shifty line of policy is far more unsafe
than a weak frontier; while it has been the last occasion
upon which English troops have joined in a campaign

with Indian allies, without retaining control of the operations. Hastings was yet at the beginning of his governorship, and this business showed that he had much to learn in high politics; for certainly his conduct betrays less than his ordinary insight into consequences and his usual skill in handling an important affair; and nowhere does Mr. Gleig, his biographer, appear so feeble as his advocate. Mr. Gleig dilates on the absurdity of holding Hastings responsible for "details of military operations" which he never sanctioned or approved; and totally fails to perceive that all men, especially men in command, are directly answerable for the indirect but probable consequences of their acts and orders. The expedition against the Rohillas was wrong in principle, for they had not provoked us, and the Vizier could only be relied upon to abuse his advantages. When Colonel Champion, who led our brigade, said that the British reputation was in the hands of the Vizier, and that the Oude army would have been routed if the British troops had not stood firm, the Calcutta Council felt the rebuke, and could only rejoin by a solemn reprimand. On the other hand, Macaulay's splendid and glittering phrases have thrown a false air of romance over the real origin and character of the Rohilla chiefships, which merely represented the fortuitous partition of an imperial province among military adventurers. In their origin, political constitution, and their relations to the bulk of the people, they might be likened to the Mamelukes of Egypt, who also were a military confederacy under a chief of their own, paying a nominal allegiance to the Sultan for a province which they had seized. And they were in reality suppressed for reasons not unlike

E

those which led to the political destruction of Poland, because their constitution was weak and turbulent, and because, therefore, they could not be trusted to hold an important position on the frontiers of more powerful States. The allegations that the country was ravaged far and wide, and that the family of Háfiz Rehmat Khan were cruelly treated by the Vizier, were investigated at the time, and were proved by evidence to be unfounded or very greatly exaggerated. The change of government did not disturb the cultivation of the lands; and although the families of the Rohilla chiefs were confined and sent away into Oude, they were treated with no other severity. The alleged depopulation of the country reduces itself, on close examination, to the banishment out of Rohilcund of about twenty thousand Rohilla Afghans found in arms, out of a population of nearly a million, including some seven hundred thousand Hindus.[1] But it must be admitted that for some years afterwards the Nawab's officers governed Rohilcund very badly, and that the people had reason to regret the able personal administration of Háfiz Rehmat Khan.

[1] Hamilton, *The Rohilla Afgans* (1787), p. 269 ; see note.

CHAPTER III

THE FIRST GOVERNOR-GENERALSHIP IN INDIA

THUS stood matters early in 1774, when the passing of the Regulating Act of 1773 had changed the constitution of the East India Company at home and of their government in India, and made Warren Hastings the first Governor-General of all our Indian territories with powers and functions defined by a Parliamentary statute. The exploits of Lord Clive whereby the Company had acquired large territorial revenues, the rumours of enormous wealth flowing into the coffers of the Company and into the pockets of its servants, the reports of scandalous misrule and corruption, had all combined to stir up the attention of the nation and of the English Ministry; and Lord Clive himself had said in the Commons that Indian affairs were very ill managed in India and in London. The Company applied to the Ministers for assistance in their financial embarrassment; Lord North was willing enough to give help, but on very hard terms. The Company's right to hold any territory was directly impugned on constitutional grounds by the English Government; although it was vigorously defended by Burke, who said that the rapine of Parliament was shaking the Company's credit. England's position in 1773 might be likened to that of some one who should

have unexpectedly inherited vast estates in remote
countries far apart from each other, and should have
discovered that their title was bad, their management
worse, that on his western estate he was being involved
in very costly and unpleasant litigation with occupants
who claimed to sit rent free, and on his eastern property
in all the troubles caused to absentee proprietors by
dishonest and incapable agency. After seven years'
contest England had won her cause both in America and
India; but in the administration of distant dependencies
she was as yet totally inexperienced, and she had to
study that difficult art through the long period of misfortune and humiliating failure into which, under Lord
North's guidance, she was just entering. That the term
of Warren Hastings' government coincided for ten years
with Lord North's premiership, is a fact to be always
remembered in appreciating the situation of the Anglo-
Indian Governor; we must take account of the inexperi-
ence of the nation, the circumstances of a troubled time,
the animosity of parties inflamed by resentments and disappointments, and the irritation of the English people.

It is useful to recollect that the tea thrown into
Boston harbour in December, 1773, belonged to the East
India Company, and had been allowed free export by
way of helping them commercially; for the incident
fixes important dates, and marks a curious point of
connection between eastern and western complications.
And while it is remarkable that a petty concession to the
Indian trading company should have been the signal
for rebellion in the American colonies, such an electric
reverberation across the horizon illustrates the tempestuous condition of the whole political atmosphere.

The state of the administration in Bengal, before the passing of Lord North's Act of 1773, is very fairly described in a letter written in November, 1773 by Warren Hastings to the Court of Directors :

" May I be permitted " (he wrote), " in all deference to your commands, to offer it as my opinion that whatever may have been the conduct of individuals, or even of the collective members of your former administrations, the blame is not so much attributable to them as to the want of a principle of government adequate to its substance and a coercive power to enforce it. The extent of Bengal and its possible resources are equal to those of most states in Europe. Its difficulties are greater than those of any, because it wants both an established form and powers of government ; it derives its actual support from the unremitted labour and personal exertions of individuals, instead of the vital influence which flows through the channels of a regular constitution. Our constitution is nowhere to be traced but in ancient charters, which were framed for the jurisdiction of your trading settlements, the rates of your exports, and the provision of your annual investment. I need not observe how incompetent these must prove for the government of a great kingdom, and for the preservation of its riches from private violence and embezzlement."

Such being the actual condition of affairs, the Act of 1773 may be regarded as the first essay by the British Parliament in constructing a regular government for India, the main object being to establish a self-acting balance of powers, and to prevent abuses by a system of co-ordinate authorities. It is necessary to give some very brief explanation of the provisions of this statute, because out of its operation arose immediately all the collisions, antagonisms, and disputes with the Council, the Court, and the two other Presidencies, by which the first Governor-General at Calcutta was so long encompassed.

The governorship of Bengal, Behar, and Orissa was vested in a Governor-General, with four Councillors, having authority over Madras and Bombay; and all correspondence relating to civil government or military affairs was to be laid by the Directors of the Company in London before His Majesty's Ministers, who could disapprove or cancel any rules or orders. A Supreme Court of Judicature, appointed by the Crown, was established in Calcutta. The Bill was opposed by Burke, who said that not one regulation of it could be supported by fair and solid arguments, though he spoke in approval of the appointment of Hastings to the Governor-Generalship. The Act was intended to set in order our Indian affairs and to terminate the confusion between conquest and commerce, by placing the country under some recognised jurisdiction and responsible authority; but in the business of administering dependencies Parliament was still, as has been said, at its apprenticeship, and the machinery of this statute was very ill contrived. The Ministers had undertaken a general supervision of the Company's proceedings, but very little direct responsibility was placed upon them for what was done. In the Governor-General's Council the opinion of the majority was made decisive in a case of differences, so that the Governor-General was liable to be entirely disabled by an adverse vote; and three of his new Councillors had been selected as the Ministers' delegates to put a curb on the Company's representatives. The Court of Judicature was completely independent of all local authority, being intended to maintain a control over the doings of the Company's servants. But as no local legislature existed, and as the laws which this court was

to administer, and their range or province, were left
uncertain, and as no tradition, precedent, or common law
of the land was at hand to guide them, the judges found
themselves practically invested with full discretion to
interpret their own authority and the prerogative of the
executive government.

Here then was a court set up with an untried and
indefinite jurisdiction over the acts of an ill-formed
hybrid Anglo-Indian government, in the midst of a very
peculiar and in some respects primitive society, that
had been morally and materially distracted by political
revolutions, and whose habits and ideas were then quite
novel to Europeans.   Upon such a people it descended,
like a new and mysterious Avatár, in the multiform
embodiment of four lawyers from Westminster Hall of
very ordinary learning and ability, wielding powers equal
or superior to the visible government, and armed with a
strange mechanical apparatus of legal formula and process quite unintelligible to Indians, and totally unsuited
to the environment.

"If," wrote Warren Hastings, in reviewing his administration eleven years later,

" If the same act of the legislature which confirmed me in
my station of President over the Company's settlements in
Bengal had invested me with a control as extensive as the
new denomination I received by it indicated ; if it had
compelled the assistance of my associates in power instead of
giving me opponents ; if, instead of creating new expectations,
which were to be accomplished by my dismission from office,
it had imposed silence on the interested clamours of faction,
and taught the servants of the Company to place their
dependence upon me, where it constitutionally rested ; if,
when it transferred the real control over the Company's
affairs from the Direction to the Ministers, instead of extend-

ing, it had limited the claims of patronage, which every man possessing influence himself, or connected with those who possessed it, thought he had a right to exert; and if it had made my continuance in office to depend on the rectitude of my intentions, and the vigour with which they were exerted, instead of annexing it to a compliance with those claims— I should have had little occasion at this period to claim the public indulgence for an avowal of duties undischarged. But the reverse took place in every instance."

Warren Hastings is here alluding to one grave consequence of the system introduced by the Act of 1773; that it rendered the aid and support of the Ministers indispensable to a Governor-General, who, if he were not connected with political parties at home, could only secure their favour and protection by placing at their disposal a large share of his Indian patronage. He had to serve not only the friends of the Directors but also the friends of the Government for the time being; and the very means employed to satisfy the party in power inevitably irritated those in opposition. The scheme itself, however, was foredoomed to miscarriage; it produced divided counsels and a discordant executive from the very beginning; nor is it matter for surprise that our first experiment in framing administrative relations between England and her Indian dominions should have signally failed. In the eighteenth century the question of governing India from London presented in their highest degree all the difficulties and enigmas inherent in the administration of dependencies that are separated from the sovereign State by distance, by differences of religion, race, climate, and by the strongest possible contrast of social ideas and political traditions. Even in the attempt to govern our American colonies,

where no such contrast existed, we blundered and failed,
though in a very different way, still more signally than
with our Asiatic conquests. And although we have
lately managed things better on the principle of allowing
self-government to outlying communities of our own
nationality, yet we are so far from having arrived at
a satisfactory solution of the problem, that the history of
the government of dependencies (which has yet to be
written) must be confessed, so far as alien races are
concerned, to be for the most part a record of failure
in all ages and countries.

Three members of Council, Francis, Clavering, and
Monson, with the Chief-Justice and Judges of the
Supreme Court, landed together at Calcutta in October,
1774; the fourth, Barwell, was a servant of the Company in India. They were landed exactly at noon
under the full glare of an Indian sun; the heat and confusion took all dignity from the procession to Government House; and Hastings had not even put on a ruffled
shirt to receive them. They accepted very coolly the
civilities of the Governor-General; and they complained
that the honours paid to them on arrival were insufficient.
The minutes and correspondence that were exchanged
on this important point show that from the moment
when Francis, Clavering, and Monson set foot in Bengal,
the quarrel began which lasted until two had died and
the third had departed to carry on the war at home.
The letter of instruction to the new government, when
formally opened by the Council thus inaugurated, was
found earnestly to recommend before all things "the
most perfect harmony among yourselves." But as it also
enjoined inquiry into past abuses, or into any dissipation

or embezzlement of the Company's money, and the application of effective remedies for such disorders, the three
Councillors acted upon this injunction without losing a
day. They called for all the confidential correspondence
that had passed between Hastings and his agent at the
Vizier's court; and when Hastings refused to produce
it, they summoned the agent to bring the papers with
him from Lucknow. They sent orders to the commandant of the Company's brigade that was still with
the Vizier of Oude, to demand immediate payment of the
forty lakhs due for assistance in expelling the Rohillas,
and to withdraw within fourteen days if the money were
not paid. They condemned the treaty of Benares under
which Allahabad had been ceded to Oude; and they
declared that the finances of Bengal had been utterly
ruined by mismanagement. In short, they reversed and
countermanded in every direction the foreign policy
of their Governor-General; and the next mail took home
a report from the Council full of complaints and accusations against him, with a long rejoinder from Hastings,
whose only adherent was Barwell.

For a government that had been opened with exhort-
ations to harmony, this was a somewhat discordant pre-
lude; and the note thus struck was diligently maintained.
When, in January, 1775, the Vizier of Oude died, the Council majority cancelled the treaties made with him, extorted
from his successor a large increase of the subsidy paid for
the Company's troops stationed in Oude, insisted on the
cession of two valuable districts, Ghazipur and Benares,
from the new Vizier, and backed up their Resident at Lucknow in upholding the claims of the late Vizier's widow,
the celebrated Bhow Begum, to retain as her personal

appanage an immense treasure and possession of certain
rich districts. The Vizier, Asaph-u-Dowlah, represented
in vain that his own mother was his inveterate enemy,
that she had detained all his father's personal property
and a vast treasure that he had accumulated, particularly
the wealth obtained from Rohilcund ; that his troops were
in mutiny and his treasury empty. He found himself
loaded with debts and losses at the beginning of his
reign ; in April, 1775, he had a pitched battle with his
refractory battalions, losing three hundred of his own
men and killing six hundred mutineers ; his mother
refused all help, declaring that she would sooner throw
her jewels and money into the river than advance the
Nawab a single rupee, and rejected the intervention of
the British Resident. The Nawab's affairs fell, as the
Resident reported, into a most distracted condition ;
and all the steps taken by the Council majority went
straight against the policy of strengthening the state
of Oude ; while as they also led up to those transactions out of which arose afterwards two of the
main charges against Hastings, it is well to remember
that he himself was so entirely opposed to them that
the majority claimed great merit with the Directors for
having carried the treaty against his remonstrances.
The Directors, in noticing these proceedings, observed with
singular satisfaction " the attention paid by our servants
to the interests of their employers." Meanwhile the
three Councillors who formed the majority had been
sedulously discharging their duty of investigating past
abuses. It is plain from a private memorandum [1] left by
Francis, that they had begun by assuming Hastings to be

---

[1] *Life of Francis,* ii. 51.

thoroughly corrupt, and went on to look for evidence
in support of a foregone conclusion. In their search
for these proofs they pulled to pieces the whole administration ; and Francis admits that they reversed his
foreign policy in order that by breaking down his
influence they might obtain some revelation of his secret
transactions.

After condemning the Governor-General's public acts,
they next proceeded to take up charges against his personal conduct. A letter from the Ráni of Burdwan, alleging that Hastings had accepted a gratification, was received
and considered by the Council. Next day appeared upon
the scene Nuncomar ; he was in politics an opportunist,
and his entry was well timed and characteristic. He
delivered to Mr. Francis, at an interview, a statement
purporting to give particulars of enormous sums received
as presents by Hastings, and setting out the causes why
he (Nuncomar) gravely suspected Hastings of corruption,
peculation, and connivance at embezzlement on a grand
scale. In a second letter, he deplored the Governor-
General's habit of preferring private emolument to the
welfare of the country, and asked leave to be heard before
the Council in support of the revelations that he had
made, which the Council by a majority at once allowed.
Several other petitions alleging dishonesty or profligate
expenditure of public money against the Governor-
General, were also received. One of them had come, as
has been said, from the Ráni of Burdwan, a lady possessing a large estate, upon whom Mr. Francis at once proposed to confer the honorary distinction usually awarded
by the Government to rank and loyalty in India. Hastings said it would be a personal indignity to the Governor-

General, but the motion was carried. The heat and fury of this mortal struggle—for Hastings had everything at stake and stood resolutely at bay—survive and still glow through the minutes of the proceedings, which appear either to have been taken down by a clerk, or to have been in some way dictated by the combatants ; and the following extract from a minute by Hastings describes his position :

" On the 13th instant, a motion was made by Colonel Monson, and supported by General Clavering and Mr. Francis, that Rajah Nuncomar should be called before the Board, and required to produce the proofs of his allegations.

" To this I strongly objected, declaring that I looked upon the members of the majority themselves as my accusers, that they were therefore unfit to sit in judgment upon me ; that I could not suffer the dignity of the First Magistrate of this Government to be debased, by sitting to be arraigned as a criminal at the Council Board, of which he was the President, by a man of character so notoriously infamous as that of Rajah Nuncomar ; and that I disclaimed their right, in any respect, to erect themselves into a tribunal to judge my conduct ; that I had no objection, and would consent to their forming themselves into a Committee for the purpose of obtaining such information as they required, but would not suffer them to bring such a business before the Board. They persisted in their purpose, and I declared the meeting dissolved."

Three times in March did the majority insist on hearing at the Council-table charges against their President. " It would appear," they recorded, " that there is no species of peculation from which the honourable Governor-General has thought it reasonable to abstain " ; and in another minute they observed that Nuncomar's discoveries explained how the honourable Governor-General had amassed about £400,000 (" which he is said to possess ") in two and a half years. Three times Hastings dissolved the sittings, repeating his offer to answer all inquiries before a committee, and withdrawing with Barwell from the Council chamber.

James Mill, who in his *History of India* twists and strains all his arguments against Hastings, cannot see why the Governor-General should have refused to preside at a Council meeting for the purpose of hearing Nuncomar accuse him of base and criminal behaviour. The reason he alleged, says Mill, was the dignity of the accused, and the baseness of the accuser; and Mill solemnly demonstrates that upon general principles these are quite inadmissible pretexts for stifling public inquiry. Mill's turn of mind was that which has been termed doctrinaire; he was rigid in his moral axioms but loose in their applications; he staked out his general principle like a net across the line of argument, and tried to drive all his victims into it. He must have seen that the objection of Hastings was only to the manner of the inquiry (for he agreed to a special committee of investigation), and as such was unanswerable, since it is hard upon any man, above all upon an Indian Governor-General, to be required to preside at his own trial. However, Hastings and Barwell departed; General Clavering took the vacant chair; Nuncomar appeared and swore he had paid large sums to the Governor, producing also a Persian letter sealed with the name of Muni Begum, and purporting to be addressed by her to Nuncomar, stating that she had given Hastings a great bribe; whereupon the three Councillors, after vainly summoning Hastings to return, then and there ordered him to refund these illegal gains, amounting to about £35,000.

If the Council majority really supposed these proceedings to be necessary or expedient in the public interest, they certainly showed themselves to be very little conversant with the business of administration. They threw themselves eagerly into the work of receiving and even suggesting accusations, confabulating with accusers, scrutinising official papers, and generally in preparing and promoting a prosecution against their chief. "Was it for this," asked Hastings, "that the legislature of Great Britain formed the new system of government in Bengal, and armed it with powers extending to every part of the British Empire in India?" It could never have been the intention of the English Ministry or the Court of Directors, when they appointed Hastings by name in the statute as Governor-General, and prescribed unity and concord as the primary condition of success, that the first use to be made of these powers should be an attempt by his colleagues to prosecute him publicly, to annul his powers, and degrade his office. They acted as if they had been sent out on a special commission to bring Hastings to trial and condign punishment upon charges of flagrant misconduct; they employed ways and means that were rash, dangerous, and unfair; and by thus suddenly pushing Hastings to the brink of ruin they made themselves largely responsible for all that ensued. They may have been persuaded that their motives were good, but their object was undoubtedly to supplant him, to drive him from the country, and to obtain the reversion of his office for one of themselves.[1] In December, 1774, Francis had been hardly two

---

[1] "The government to me was then (1773 ?) an object out of all view and contemplation. The idea of its being by any possibility

months in India, and probably all three Councillors had much under-estimated the character of the man whom they were attacking. Francis wrote to Lord North in February, 1775, that, "without denying him (Hastings) some little talents of the third or fourth order, we were as much deceived with regard to his abilities and judgments as to his other qualifications. I look back to my own prepossessions in his favour as to a sort of delirium, from which he himself has recovered me."

But events very speedily showed that the real hallucination of the Councillors lay in a different quarter. Within a month from the time when Nuncomar had tendered his accusations against Hastings, Hastings prosecuted Nuncomar and others for conspiracy. They were charged with having forced one Kamál-u-Din by threats and menaces to present to the Council a petition falsely accusing the Governor-General of divers enormous and scandalous offences; and the judges, after examining witnesses, held Nuncomar and two others to bail. It was evident that Hastings had his back to the wall and was now fairly crossing swords with his antagonists, for by this prosecution he struck directly at Nuncomar; and the Councillors ranged themselves openly behind the man whom they were backing. They all went to visit Nuncomar, thereby paying him a very unusual official compliment, "as an innocent man and the victim of State policy"; they entertained fresh charges of peculation, and enlarged the scope of their investigations. Three weeks later, on May 6th, came the arrest of

attainable never occurred to me till December, 1774, when Clavering informed me of his resolution to decline the succession himself."— Memorandum by Francis, *Life,* ii. 48.

Nuncomar on the famous charge of forging and publish-
ing a bond, upon the information of one Mohun Persád,
an old and bitter enemy with whom he had a lawsuit;
when the judges, after a hearing that lasted twelve
hours, committed Nuncomar to the common jail. Meanwhile Muni Begum had disowned as a fabrication the
letter to Nuncomar which he had produced; whereupon
she was at once turned out of her guardianship by the
Council, who appointed Nuncomar's son in her stead.
The vigour and rapidity with which these home-thrusts
were exchanged between the antagonists is very remarkable; it is as if they were fiercely fighting hand to hand.
Hastings resembles a man suddenly set upon by his
enemies, when the swords clash together, and he defends
himself until at a critical moment some friendly rapier
runs his foremost assailant right through the body.
Mohun Persád's charge came so opportunely and
decisively that Hastings' enemies unhesitatingly accused
him of instigating it; Burke and Francis stamped the
imputation upon him with unwearied reiteration; and
it has become an article of popular belief since Macaulay
declared that no one but an idiot or a biographer ever
doubted its truth. Nuncomar wrote to the Council on
his commitment, that the consequence of having incurred
the Governor-General's resentment appeared in his letter
being dated from the common jail, and prayed for interposition in his behalf. But during the course of the
trial no such imputation was suggested; and although
the point has been argued on both sides with much
ability, minuteness, and acrimony, there is in fact no
tangible ground for denying that the prosecution originated in an ordinary and regular way, out of a civil suit

F

that had been going on for two years, until on the establishment of the Supreme Court Mohun Persád's attorney advised criminal proceedings.

Nuncomar prayed the Council to intercede for his transfer to a less irksome place of imprisonment, pleading that his caste and health were imperilled in the jail, and General Clavering laid stress on the importance to the public of the life of a man who could prove a Governor-General's venality. But the Chief-Justice, after sending an English physician to make inquiry, and after consulting the Pundits, merely ordered that his confinement should be made as easy as possible. His trial began before an English jury on June 8th, and lasted until the 16th; the heat must have been at its maximum in Calcutta, yet the judges wore their heavy wigs continually, that no forms might be wanting. The alleged forgery arose out of a transaction of thirteen years before, and the fact, if true, must have been long known to the complainant. The witnesses to the bond were dead: the hostility of Mohun Persád to Nuncomar was notorious; and it has been thought then and since that upon the evidence for the prosecution, taken alone, the accused might have escaped conviction, if a maladroit question put by Nuncomar to one of his own witnesses had not led to further questions by the judges under which the witness broke down. The prisoner was convicted: his application for leave to appeal was summarily rejected by the judge; and when his advocate presented a petition for respite of sentence, which one juryman had been induced to sign, he only elicited a harsh rebuke from Impey, who was offended at Nuncomar being described as an unhappy victim. Moreover, it has been clearly

shown that when Clavering, Monson, and Francis were
asked, as representing the executive government, to
intercede with the Court for a respite, they refused on
the ground that the business had no relation to the
public concerns of the country. A pathetic letter to
Francis from Nuncomar himself, imploring his interposition, seems to have had no answer at all, and a
few days afterwards he was executed.

Sir James Stephen, in his excellent book on Nuncomar
and Impey, has explained that Macaulay's vivid picture
of the execution, which has become historic, was mainly
drawn from a description written by the sheriff who super-
intended the proceedings. The moment of dying brings
out the strong points of a high-caste Hindu's faith and
character; whatever his life may have been, he always
faces death steadily, and Nuncomar suffered with compos-
ure and fortitude. He had played the game of politics in
his own way, after the manner of his time, and he probably
thought that he had been fairly beaten with his own
weapons. Nor is it likely that his feelings at paying
forfeit were more bitter than those of many a man who
in other countries and ages has staked his life upon some
dangerous and unscrupulous plot against a powerful
adversary. The public hanging of a man of Nuncomar's
caste, age, and rank for such an offence as forgery
undoubtedly shocked the sentiments of the native
spectators, and the rigour of the punishment amounted
to injustice. But Macaulay, who followed Sir Gilbert
Elliot's speech on Impey's impeachment, has exaggerated
the horror and dismay caused by the execution; for it
must be remembered that India had for centuries been
under rulers who had left the Hindus no reason whatever

for supposing that the sanctity of a Brahmin's life would be respected by foreign judges or governors.

Some days after Nuncomar's death General Clavering produced in Council a letter to himself, in which Nuncomar declared that those whom he had accused before the Council were destroying him to save themselves, being aided and abetted by the judges who had unjustly condemned him. Upon a proposal made by Hastings that this letter should be transmitted to the judges, Francis said that it contained insinuations that were wholly unsupported and libellous, and that it ought to be burned by the common hangman. The petition was expunged from the Council's record; but Hastings privately sent a copy to the Chief-Justice, who produced it in defending himself at the bar of the House of Commons. When Francis had afterwards to reconcile this conduct with his vehement assertions that Hastings and Impey had conspired to commit the judicial murder of Nuncomar, he could only allege that this secret giving of an official paper proved an understanding between them, and that the Council majority were in mortal fear of judges who had already dipped their hands in blood, and who were manifestly at the Governor-General's disposal. But although it does seem that they were startled and silenced for the time by Nuncomar's fate, yet if at the moment they verily believed Nuncomar to have died by foul play, three such men as Clavering, Monson, and Francis could scarcely have been so base and fainthearted as to treat his last appeal with ignominy and simulated disdain.

It may perhaps be said that no trial has been so often tried over again by such diverse authorities, or in so many different ways, as this celebrated proceeding. During the course of a century it has been made the theme of historical, political, and biographical discussions; all the points have been argued and debated by great orators and great lawyers; it has formed the avowed basis of a motion in Parliament to impeach the Chief-Justice, and it must have weighed heavily, though indirectly, with those who decided to impeach the Governor-General. It gave rise to rumours of a dark and nefarious conspiracy which, whether authentic or not, exactly suited the humour and the rhetoric of some contemporary English politicians. Two Lord Chancellors have commented on it; and it has furnished an apparently inexhaustible subject for literary criticism and sharp-edged controversy over the smallest details. The present writer will therefore be readily excused for not attempting to enter far upon such well-trodden ground.

Very recently Sir James Stephen, after subjecting the whole case to exact scrutiny and the most skilful analysis, after examining every document and every fact bearing upon this matter with anxious attention, has pronounced judgment declaring that Nuncomar's trial was perfectly fair, that Hastings had nothing to do with the prosecution, and that at the time there was no sort of conspiracy or understanding between Hastings and Impey in relation to it. Nothing can be more masterly or more effective than the method employed by Sir James Stephen to explode and demolish, by the force of a carefully-laid train of proofs, the loose fabric of assertions, invectives, and ill-woven demonstrations upon which the enemies of Hastings and Impey based and pushed forward their attacks, and which have never before been so vigorously battered in reply. The rancour of the language used by such men as Sir Gilbert Elliot and all the leading managers of the impeachment, is only equalled by its carelessness; it illustrates a stormy Parliamentary atmosphere and a generally low range of the political barometer, which go far to account for the misfortunes of those who, like Hastings, were exposed to the violence of parties.

It may be accepted, upon Sir James Stephen's authority, that no evidence can be produced to justify conclusions adverse to the innocence of Hastings upon a charge that has from its nature affected the popular tradition regarding him far more deeply than the accusations of high-handed oppressive political transactions, which are little understood and leniently condemned by the English at large. There is really nothing to prove that he had anything to do with the prosecution, or that he influenced the sentence; for the circumstances which have been strung together to support the belief in his guilt are all reconcilable with a theory of his innocence. They merely explain the rumour; they are like the scattered incidents that may be faint indications of a true historic event, or may only account for the formation of a myth. Nevertheless when Sir James Stephen undertakes to establish, by argument drawn from the general motives of human action, the moral certainty that Hastings was totally unconnected with the business, and that the popular impression against him is utterly wrong, his demonstration is necessarily less conclusive, and we may reasonably hesitate about standing surety to this extent for the undiscoverable

motives and behaviour of a man in the situation of
Hastings. With his reticence, self-command, consummate mastery of his instruments, fertility of resource,
and firmness of purpose, he was not likely to blunder in
such a simple, easy, and yet dangerous movement as
would be required to set going the prosecution without leaving traces that might lead to his detection in
after years. "He was," observes Sir James Stephen,
"apparently a curiously cautious, secret man." The
fact remains unshaken that Nuncomar tried to ruin the
Governor-General, and would probably have succeeded
if he himself had not been instantaneously crushed; nor
is it easy to agree with Sir James Stephen's view that
Hastings, by interfering in the prosecution, incurred
a tremendous risk of utter ruin for no reason at all.
If the Governor-General desired to encourage or promote a prosecution against a man who was known to
have come within the four corners of the English law,
he could undoubtedly have conveyed an intimation to
Mohun Persád with little or no risk of discovery; and
the fact that Impey tried the man with great patience,
forbearance, and exact formality, might prove nothing
against an intention to hang him, but only that he was
too wise to strain the law superfluously. On the whole
there is no reason whatever to dissent from Pitt's view,
who treated the accusation of a conspiracy between
Impey and Hastings for the purpose of destroying
Nuncomar, as destitute of any shadow of solid proof.
Whether Hastings, when Nuncomar openly tried to
ruin him by false and malignant accusations, became
aware and made use in self-defence of the fact that his
accuser had rendered himself liable to a prosecution for

forgery, is a different question, upon which also no evidence exists or is likely to be forthcoming. But if a hint
to prosecute could rid the Governor-General of a formidable and treacherous enemy, it is by no means improbable
that he may have thought himself warranted in deliver-
ing so opportune and decisive a counter-stroke ; and most
men of his stamp would have done likewise.

There can be no doubt that Nuncomar's arrest had
sharply checked the combined attack upon Hastings ;
its leader was suddenly struck down as by a chance shot,
and the Governor-General had time to rally his spirits
for an obstinate resistance. The state of his mind may
be seen in a letter which he previously wrote in March to
Lord North :

"I now most earnestly entreat that your Lordship—for
on you, I presume, it finally rests—will free me from the
state I am in, either by my immediate recall, or by the
confirmation of the trust and authority of which you have
hitherto thought me deserving, on such a footing as shall
enable me to fulfil your expectations, and to discharge the
debt which I owe to your Lordship, to my country, and my
Sovereign.

"The meanest drudge, who owes his daily subsistence to
daily labour, enjoys a condition of happiness compared to
mine, while I am doomed to share the responsibility of
measures which I disapprove, and to be an idle spectator of
the ruin which I cannot avert."

On the same day he wrote to his agent in England,
Colonel Macleane, and to another friend, that he had
resolved to return to England by the first ship of the
next season, if the first advices from England should
contain a disapprobation of the treaty of Benares, or of
the Rohilla war, and should mark an evident disinclina-
tion against him. He left it to their discretion to make

such use of this resolution as they should think proper.
His next letter of April 29th to the same persons,
as given by Mr. Gleig, contains no further allusion to
this resolution. It is written at the climax of the storm
of accusations against which he is striving, when his
adversaries are closing round him, and when his Council
have sent home a despatch reporting that he is universally condemned in India as a guilty man. On
May 18th, however, he writes a third letter in a very
different tone. Nuncomar is in jail "and in a fair way
to be hanged"; he entreats his correspondents to study
carefully the official papers that are sent to them in
order that they may understand the course of events
during the last month; and in a postscript he retracts
the resolution communicated to them on March 27th.
The whole tenor of this letter expresses a conviction
that upon full information the authorities at home will
support him against the majority, and that "men whose
actions are so frantic will not be permitted to remain in
charge of so important a trust." He evidently thought
that the eager hostility of his assailants had carried them
too far; but though it is plain that he regarded Nuncomar's imprisonment as a triumph, this attitude is too
natural in his situation to throw any light upon the
question whether he himself had any surreptitious share
in his enemy's discomfiture. The minutes of September,
1775, evidently commemorate a fierce encounter. The
Governor-General charges the majority with employing
declamation and invective against him. They reply that
they have used neither, but rely on proofs, positive and
presumptive; and they add that after the death of
Nuncomar "the Governor is well assured that no man

who regards his own safety will stand forward as his
accuser." To which Hastings rejoins in these words
only : " I have declared on oath before the Supreme
Court that I neither advised nor encouraged the prosecution of Maharajah Nuncomar. It would have ill become
the first magistrate in the settlement to have employed
his influence either to promote or dissuade it."

The disputes and open hostilities between the two
parties in the Council continued throughout the following twelve months, and spread into every transaction of
the government. The majority proceeded to reverse
all the acts that had been made by Warren Hastings
as Governor before their arrival. He had, as will be
remembered, gradually discontinued the system of
double government whereby the criminal jurisdiction
was left with the native officers of the titular Nawab of
Bengal, by introducing regular courts in their room ;
and he had removed Mahomed Reza Khan, who had
been the chief native administrator under that system.
The Council majority now abolished the new provincial
courts, restored the jurisdiction of the Nawab, and reappointed Mahomed Reza. In regard to foreign affairs
the policy of the Council majority towards the Oude
Vizier had proved ruinous to their ally ; for owing to his
mutinous army, his powerful and intractable mother,
and the incessant demands made on him by the British
Resident for arrears of debt, Asaph-u-Dowlah's predicament was most distressful ; and the whole country
appears, by the description given in the letters from
the Resident at Lucknow, to have been falling away
into masterless confusion. On the western side of India
the Company's government at Bombay had taken posses-

sion of Salsette Island, and in order to secure their acquisition they had formed an alliance with a Mahratta chief named Ragoba, and had sent a body of troops to support his attempt to reinstate himself in power at Poona, where he had formerly usurped the rulership but had been since expelled. As the Bombay authorities in thus beginning a war without sanction from Calcutta had exceeded their power, and as the expedition was in itself rash and impolitic, the Governor-General in Council sent orders conveying strong disapproval, and desiring that all military operations should be stopped. But the Bombay government so vehemently represented the military and political objections against an abrupt cessation of hostilities, that Hastings thought they had gone too far to break off with honour or safety, and must be allowed to carry through the business up to a point where they might decently get out of it. The expedition was badly conducted and signally unsuccessful; it very nearly came to a disastrous end, although the English managed to keep Salsette. The Council naturally threw on Warren Hastings all the responsibility of having refused to insist peremptorily on the withdrawal of our troops, and in this transaction Burke subsequently found material for one of his sharpest charges.

Affairs in the Madras Presidency went on no better than in Calcutta or Bombay. The Nawab of the Carnatic desired to seize the possessions and property of the Rajah of Tanjore, a tributary chief, with whom the Company had made a treaty some years earlier. The Madras government at first disapproved of the Nawab's intention, but very soon afterwards took part with him, and sent troops to aid the Nawab in an attack

on the Rajah, who was subdued and imprisoned. As
this was in direct contravention of instructions that
had been given by the Court of Directors, they dismissed the Madras governor, and Lord Pigot was
sent out to replace him and to set matters right. He
accordingly proceeded to restore the Rajah of Tanjore,
but in the meantime the Nawab of the Carnatic had
made large assignments of the Tanjore revenue to the
notorious Paul Benfield and others, who were not disposed to lose their securities, and who had friends in
Council. So Lord Pigot found himself, like Hastings,
in a minority ; and when he attempted to carry his own
measures with a high hand, he was arrested by order
of the major party, whose authority was obeyed by the
army ; he was thrown into jail, and there died before
the orders from England to release and recall him could
arrive. The Council at Calcutta, holding that all power
vested in a majority, and undismayed by this somewhat
extreme and truculent application of the principle, naturally supported their brethren at Madras, and on this
occasion they were joined by Hastings, who might certainly have shown more fellow-feeling for the troubles
of a governor beset by vindictive councillors. It must
be supposed that he believed himself obliged to disown
Lord Pigot's imprudent attempt to override the legal
limits of a governor's authority ; for he had never
allowed the heat of his own conflict with his Council
to draw him into a similar predicament. The Bombay
government sympathised with Lord Pigot ; the Court
of Directors, in high indignation, dismissed all the members of Council, and ordered the military officers who
had arrested the governor to be tried by court-martial.

It must be admitted that the new system of governing our Indian possessions had not, up to this time, fulfilled the objects of establishing harmony and a firm, efficacious administration. The relations of the Presidency governors and the different native States of India were still undoubtedly uncertain, ill-defined, irregular, and not to be controlled from Calcutta without great risk of serious complications and misunderstandings, owing to distance and difficulty of communications. The Council of the Governor-General was distracted by violent internal animosities, and was only united in open hostilities against the Supreme Court of Judicature; the minor governments were insubordinate, having both entangled themselves in unjust and rather disreputable wars; while in London the governing body was enfeebled and dislocated by antagonistic interests and intrigues. Under the system of party warfare, as it was waged in England at the end of the eighteenth century, patronage was essential to political predominance, for a decisive superiority in this arm was to the Minister what the possession of a strong arsenal is to a commander in the field; and as Indian appointments offered unlimited resources to a hard-fighting Cabinet it was this as much as anything else that brought Indian affairs within the Parliamentary arena. Lord North seems to have contemplated taking formal possession, in the Crown's name, of all the Company's Indian territory; a measure which Hastings, whose ideas constantly anticipated long subsequent events, had at one time been grievously suspected by the Company of favouring. Lord North certainly endeavoured to retain a preponderating influence, through his nominees, over the Court of Directors in London and the Council in Calcutta; he wished to set aside Hastings and to replace him by General Clavering, who had some Parliamentary connection. To these views and intentions a powerful opposition was made by the East India Company, who had their own advocates in the House of Commons, and who denounced the proposed assumption of sovereignty as a tyrannical confiscation of private property. Thus the conflict of parties, the clashing of interests, and the anarchy produced by the ridiculous constitution of the local Indian governments, prevented the establishment of any definite policy or plan of administration in the conduct of Indian affairs.

Men appointed to govern distant and unsettled provinces, inhabited and surrounded by alien races, are more like naval commanders on the high sea than constitutional governors. There is no power of reference to public opinion or to headquarters; if the steering is by votes of the ship's officers it will run a very tortuous course. All these diverse elements of weakness and confusion combined to encompass Hastings, to deprive him of support upon very slippery ground, to strew his path with obstacles, and greatly to increase the risk of any false step.

The feud between the Governor-General in Council and the judges in Calcutta arose inevitably out of the vague character of the Court's jurisdiction, as expressed by the Act and the Charter. The wording of these instruments reflected the hesitation and irresolution of the legislators, who were in truth unable to make up their minds upon certain cardinal points, because they were not yet prepared by accurate knowledge of facts or by experience to undertake the construction of a scheme of judicature adapted to the peculiar needs of a situation that had no precedent in the constitutional history of the kingdom. In the first place, the provinces of the executive government and the Supreme Court respectively were left without clear demarcation, and every communication between them left each party in a highly electrical condition. The Court heard that the Council had recorded on their minutes something disparaging to their body, and demanded a copy of the record. The Council refuse, whereupon the judges threaten the Council with the utmost rigour of the law against defamation, and paraphrase Horace for their benefit by declaring— "Just and tenacious of the great purpose for which it was His Majesty's pleasure to send us to this country, neither the tumultuous clamour of the multitude nor the angry frown of authority shall ever move us." In the second place, it was impossible to determine, and it has always been doubted, how far, and with what qualifications, the Court's jurisdiction could be exercised throughout the districts which paid revenue to the Company, and particularly whether the judges had power to review and control the proceedings of the Company's district courts, and of its revenue administration, including the zemindars.

There have been times in the annals of every country when powerful classes and interests have been greatly concerned in avoiding any precise declaration of the public law, and when all title-deeds are so irregular that no one cares to demand a scrutiny. No one as yet ventured openly to assume the sovereignty of our Indian acquisitions ; so that all our first projects of constructive administration were affected by this instability

at their base. Hastings, with his usual clear-headed
boldness, desired to throw aside the pretext of governing in the name of the titular Nawab of Bengal, believing
that it merely caused uncertainty and embarrassment.
His view was supported by a ruling of the judges, who
refused to recognise any sovereignty in the Nawab; but
the Council majority were against him. In discussing
the Court's rule Hastings said openly that "no subtleties
or distinctions of political sophistry will conceal the
possession of power where it is universally exercised and
felt in its operation"; and he proposed that, unless
instructions to the contrary should be received, "we do
stand forth in the name of the Company as the actual
Government of these Provinces, and assume the exercise
of it in every instance without concealment of partici-
pation." Ten years later this was actually done, and
every one now agrees that Hastings was right; but in
1775 Francis and others outvoted him, so the confusion
of fictitious jurisdictions continued.

The Supreme Court finally determined not to decide
the point whether the king was or was not sovereign
of Bengal, holding that Parliament had cautiously
avoided it.

Sir James Stephen gives, in his book upon Nuncomar
and Impey, a very accurate and complete account of the
quarrel between the Court and the Council, with a full
explanation of the issues between them. It may be
sufficient here to say that the Court, while admitting
that the administration of the country was vested in the
Governor-General and Council, claimed and exercised
authority to entertain actions against all persons in the
Company's service, and also against the zemindars who

held the land and were constructively employed in the collection of its revenues. Any administrative act or order might thus be, and many were, challenged, and had to satisfy the forms and procedure of Westminster Hall. The Council thereupon declared that the whole machinery of the public business was at a standstill when officers were at any moment exposed to ruinous and vexatious prosecutions; that the Court was usurping, without warrant, all the real power in the country, and that there was scarcely any sort of government, however necessary and expedient, that did not expose its highest officials to suits against them in the Supreme Court. The judges rejoined to the effect that their first duty was to protect the people from official oppression; that nowhere was such oppression more notoriously rife than in the collection of land revenue; that the real objection of the Company's servants and the zemindars was to being made answerable to any law at all; and that, as for the Court's jurisdiction, the Court alone could define it. The conflict of jurisdictions is an inevitable stage in the early political organisation of all States, as soon as the great departments of public business begin to take their proper shape; and it was sure to arise on the first establishment of the co-ordinate authorities in a distant province with no sovereign power present on the spot to arbitrate between them. When such disputes reached their climax they could only be decided by force, and on one well-known occasion the Sheriff of Calcutta, with an armed force, was opposed and arrested by the Company's sepoys. Nor was this by any means the last instance of resistance by the Indian executive to a writ of the Supreme Court, for similar controversies have since been frequently renewed. But a hundred years ago the art of adjusting English institutions to the necessary conditions of their existence in a totally different climate was little understood; the science of jurisprudence had not taken up such problems; there was great ambiguity about the law, and in practice each side tried to reduce the other's claims to an absurdity. Burke admitted that our territorial acquisitions in India were of a new and peculiar description, unknown to the ancient constitution of England, and held on anomalous tenures not easily brought within the verge of English jurisprudence. It may be added that the institutions which we imported into India were equally strange and incomprehensible by the light of Asiatic statecraft, for under all native governments, supreme or subordinate, the ultimate judicial and executive powers were still so closely united in the same persons that their deliberate disjunction in Bengal must have seemed to the people a device of extraordinary fatuity, contrary to the first principles of political mechanics. When, therefore, a revenue officer, acting under the orders of the Governor-General in Council, enforced some process of coercion against a revenue defaulter, and immediately found himself served with a writ from the Supreme Court which compelled him to defend an action in Calcutta some hundred miles away, or to be arrested and imprisoned if he did not obey—such a dilemma puzzled the people and seemed amazing to them. The rough arbitrary system of revenue collection which the English had taken over from the native government was often used oppressively and corruptly; but the device of correcting it by actions at law and arrests on "mesne process" only increased the confusion. The truth is that outside Calcutta there were at that time no laws at all, while the government had no power and not much inclination to make any ; so that in the provinces the administration of justice was in a condition not unlike that of Ireland under the Tudors, when the Lord Justices dispensed English law within the pale, and beyond it neither held their own courts nor recognised any other jurisdiction.

During the earlier period of the quarrel between the Court and the Council, Hastings, standing apart from his colleagues, maintained his intimacy with Impey and endeavoured to concert remedies for the manifest evils and defects of this situation. He admitted that the revenue officers had often acted oppressively, and that the Court's protection had been useful to the people; and with his usual acuteness he proposed a plan that cut at the root of the matter.

"The truth is," he wrote, "that a thing done by halves is worse done than if it were not done at all. The powers of the Court must be universal or it would be better to repeal them altogether. The attempt to make distinctions has introduced the most glaring absurdities and contradictions into an Act which virtually declares the British sovereignty over the provinces even in the qualifications which are used to limit it."

The measures proposed by Hastings for quieting all these disputes and uncertainties were certainly broad and drawn upon an ample scale. It may be gathered from his correspondence that during the year 1776 he sent home proposals for placing all Bengal openly under British sovereignty to be exercised through the Company ; and that he would have given the Supreme Court full control over all the provincial courts of justice, thus abolishing all these troublesome and unintelligible distinctions and limitations of jurisdiction. With the native states whose alliance might be desirable, he would have concluded engagements in the name of the Crown in order to give strength and dignity to the connexion. In communicating his plans to Lord North, on whose support he very erroneously counted, he mentioned that Sir Elijah Impey approved them, and he intimated that he had no complaint to make against the attitude of the Court towards the government. No one can deny that Warren Hastings possessed, to a degree rare at that period, the talent of political organisation; for his projects, though premature, were all sketched out on the lines that have been subsequently followed in building up our Indian empire. He saw that the old political fabric was too completely ruined to serve any longer even the purpose of a convenient fiction; he proposed to pull it down and to reconstruct it upon the foundation of facts. In the following passages he takes a rapid and comprehensive survey of the situation, given so briefly that it may be worth extracting:

" On my arrival in Bengal, I found this government in possession of a great and rich dominion, and a wide political system which has been since greatly extended, without one rule of government but what descended to it from its ancient commercial institutions, or any principle of policy but such as accident or the desultory judgment of those in actual power recommended. It was necessary to restore the authority of government to the source from which its powers originated; to assume the direct control instead of allowing it to act by a concealed and weakened influence ; to constitute an uniform and effectual mode for the management and collection of the public revenue ; to establish regular courts for the adminis-

tration of civil and criminal justice ; to give strength and
utility to its political connexions, and to transfer a share of its
wealth to Great Britain without exhausting its circulation."

The last words of this extract must not be overlooked,
for they indicate one large source of all the troubles
against which Hastings, less fortunate than his successors,
had to contend. It was not sufficient in those days that
the administration of our transmarine possessions in any
part of the world should be solvent, and should lay no
burden on the imperial exchequer—they were also expected to yield a certain profit, fiscal or commercial, to
Great Britain. And while such was the general principle
of our colonial policy, no one doubted that our Indian possessions, acquired and held under a trading charter, ought
to pay interest on the investment.   In those days Indian
commerce not only followed but carried the flag; and
conquest was still treated as a subordinate and incidental
contingency.   In the present time this position has become reversed; for although the struggle among the great
trading nations of the world is as keen as ever, it is now
not conquest that is made under cover of commercial
enterprise, but commerce that pushes forward and occu-
pies fresh territory upon considerations, more or less
genuine, of political expediency.   Warren Hastings,
indeed, was the last Governor-General who had to find
dividends out of revenue, or could be censured for dis-
sipating in wars and subsidies the money that should
have been employed in buying produce for export to the
home markets.

Up to the middle of the year 1776 Hastings continued
to make head against foes in Council at Calcutta, and a
strong adverse party at home.   Francis wrote home

despondently, in March, 1776, that while Monson and Clavering were in woful plight from sickness, and Barwell only alive because death did not think him worth taking, Hastings was "much more tough than any of us, and will never die a natural death." Francis himself was losing spirits and health; insomuch that Impey, who hated him profoundly, prophesied that if Hastings should be removed, "Francis will be with God before the news arrives." In strife and sickness they worked on until at last the death of Colonel Monson in September, 1776, gave the Governor-General predominance in Council; for his casting vote, with Barwell's steady adherence, threw Clavering and Francis into the minority. The lead thus obtained Hastings never afterwards relinquished, so that the whole of his long subsequent administration bears the full impress of his character. He lost no time in turning out Bristow, who had been sent by the Council majority to the important post of Resident at the Court of Oude, and in reinstating Middleton, his own original nominee. Everything now depended on the choice of Monson's successor. Sir Elijah Impey wrote to Lord Thurlow proposing himself for the vacancy, and Hastings naturally showed much anxiety about the matter. Yet in a letter to his English agent he declared characteristically that even if a hostile colleague were sent out, and the scales were then again turned against him, nothing but death or the king's direct order should dislodge him from the Governor-Generalship.

This determination was very soon put to a sharp and sudden test. While Hastings, no longer checked by the adverse party in Council, was laying out and pressing onward his plans of administrative reform, and was pur-

suing his policy of consolidating a system of alliance with
the leading native powers, his resignation of the Governor-
Generalship had been tendered and accepted in London.
We have seen [1] that in March, 1775, when encompassed and
driven to bay by assailants and accusers, he had formally
announced to his friends who acted for him at home
that if the Rohilla war and his treaty with Oude should
be condemned at headquarters, he should at once leave
India. It may be laid down as an axiom that if a man
determines twelve months beforehand what step he will
take in an important contingency, he will certainly
repent of his pledge when he is called upon to fulfil it ;
but Hastings at Calcutta was forced to trust much to his
London agents, and in this as in another still more
serious matter he suffered greatly from the zeal of his
friends. The Court of Directors did in fact pass a guarded
kind of censure upon the Rohilla war ; nevertheless
when in 1776 the question arose of removing Hastings
from the Governor-Generalship, the real motive was not
so much disapproval of his policy as desire for his place.
Clavering and Francis, who both hoped to succeed
Hastings, had spared no pains to damage his reputation
with their Parliamentary friends, and a strong party in
the India House, backed by Ministerial instigations, was
formed to carry a vote of recall. In the Court of
Directors it was passed by a majority of one, and although
it was rescinded by a large majority in the Court of Proprietors, Colonel Macleane, seeing Hastings threatened
with prosecutions, and supposing that his principal
wished to secure an honourable retreat from a precarious
position, sent in on his behalf a resignation of the

[1] Pages 72, 73.

Governor-Generalship on the understanding that he
retired with honour and with complete indemnity from
all future molestation. The Directors accepted the compromise and reported to the Ministers that Mr. Hastings
desired to resign. Mr. Wheler was nominated to succeed
him, and Clavering, who was gazetted to the Bath, was
appointed to hold office *ad interim* until Wheler should
arrive.

In June, 1777, despatches reached Calcutta communicating these changes to the Council, where the altercations
between Hastings and Clavering had recently revived—
as Francis wrote, and as the minutes of proceedings
amply testify—"with redoubled bitterness and fury."
"Our superiors," Hastings truly observed, "will have long
since ceased to look in our consultations for temperate
and friendly communications in the search of truth."
If, indeed, they had looked into those papers for some
clue to what was going on, they might have gathered it
from the cool and cutting replies by Hastings to the
violent and vain protests of the minority against "acts
of despotism that would disgrace even the government
of Morocco." He had turned the tables on his enemies,
and was not the man to waste his opportunity.

In this atmosphere of heat and exasperation the effect
produced by the arrival in Calcutta of the orders re-
placing Hastings by Clavering may easily be imagined.
The opening of the despatches produced an immediate
explosion. The Council chamber became the scene of an
exciting but not very dignified contest between Hastings
who, supported by Barwell, refused to give up office,
and Clavering who, backed by Francis, took the oaths
as Governor-General *ad interim*, seized the despatches

from Europe, and demanded the keys of the fort and
treasuries. Each party seems to have presided and
deliberated at a separate table, exchanging point blank
minutes and issuing contradictory orders. Clavering
ordered the commandant of the fort to obey him.
Hastings directed him to refuse obedience, and the
commandant stood by Hastings, who, as Macaulay
notices, was always popular with the army. Hastings
appealed to the judges. Clavering agreed to await their
decision; and the judges, like the army, took the side
of Hastings, deciding without loss of time positively and
unanimously against Clavering. Sir James Stephen
believes that when Hastings wrote long afterwards that
he was "at one time indebted to Impey's support for
the safety of his fortune, honour, and reputation," the
allusion was to the services rendered him by the judges
on this occasion; not, as Macaulay assumes confidently,
to the trial of Nuncomar. But the words certainly read
more like a reference to some confidential transaction
than to such a public and formal proceeding as the
Court's finding upon a case submitted for opinion. On
the other hand, Hastings could hold his tongue so well,
that if Impey had really connived with him to hang
Nuncomar, it is almost incredible that he should have
alluded in this passing way to such a secret; although
he might have alluded to Impey's support in the matter
if it had been given without any collusion or private
understanding. Moreover, the award of the judges in
1777 did undoubtedly save Hastings from official annihilation, since if at that moment he had been compelled
by an adverse decree to make room for his enemies, he
would have been utterly abandoned and driven into

obscurity; for the grounds upon which he maintained that his resignation had been unauthorised or at any rate subsequently revoked would hardly have satisfied the Ministers at home. With the Court at his back he triumphed easily. He was now able to retaliate by declaring that Clavering in his haste to become Governor-General had vacated his own Councillorship, and was thus officially in the air; but even Francis saw that there had been too much heat and precipitation. There was a general agreement to drop the business, and two months later Sir John Clavering died.

When the letters of Clavering and Francis, reporting that Hastings had not only refused to resign but had tried to dismiss General Clavering, reached England, George the Third was highly indignant at this "daring step," and wrote to Lord North that the dignity of Parliament would be annihilated if Hastings, Barwell, and the judges were not all removed. But the East India proprietors stood by Hastings, discerning him to be the best man for their interests in a stormy time. Burgoyne had surrendered at Saratoga: the French had just declared war; and on the whole the Ministers could not venture to send out a new and untried Governor-General to India. So Warren Hastings was now supreme in the Calcutta Council, for Mr. Wheler, who succeeded Clavering, was a man of no weight; and Sir Eyre Coote, who arrived later as the military member, did not oppose him systematically. The measures which he carried about this time are worth notice as showing how much of our present administrative methods and of our political system in India is due to his initiation. He established, against strenuous opposition by Francis in Council, and notwithstanding

the disapprobation of the Court of Directors, an office
for inquiring into and fixing the rateable value of lands
in Bengal, and for recording the rights and tenures of
the cultivating and landowning classes. Such investigations have always been exceedingly unpopular with the
class that is interested in defeating them ; but from
the days of the Roman empire (when settlements were
made on a system very similar to that of modern India)
the careful valuation of land and record of tenure have
always formed the essential basis of assessments under a
government that depended on the land revenue. In
India this system had fallen into desuetude until Hastings
revived and readjusted it, and the example which he
thus set has been followed everywhere in British India,
though unluckily Lord Cornwallis thought to improve
on it by making the assessment permanent in Bengal.
The second measure passed by Hastings was the transfer
of the disciplined troops maintained under treaty by the
Nawab of Oude to the service of the Company, who
undertook to pay and command them in exchange for
an assignment of land revenue equal to their cost.
Hastings described this as little more than a change of
form to provide for regular payment and proper discipline of a soldiery whom the Nawab kept in a chronic
state of mutiny. But it was the formal beginning of
that remarkable and extensive organisation of subsidised
forces and contingents, which has played a curious part
in our Indian wars and treaties, which is an element of
insecurity as well as of strength, and which may yet enter
upon some new phase in our calculations of the collected
military resources of the empire.

But it is possible that Hastings did not sufficiently

remember that with irresistible authority comes also full
personal responsibility. Although Francis, the sole
survivor of the three hostile Councillors, could no longer
thwart him in India, he could still inflame and heap
fuel on all the resentments and animosities that were
accumulating against him at home ; while Hastings, con-
fident in his own superior capacity and knowledge of
Indian affairs, and in his rising reputation and popularity
in Bengal, was triumphantly overriding objections to his
plans and policy. Out of the events and transactions
of the period into which he was now entering arose all
the charges that were afterwards most heavily pressed
against him by the Committee of Impeachment. It is of
little use at the present time to discuss critically the
motives by which the Governor-General was actuated
in continuing the war with the Mahrattas, in which the
Bombay government had so recklessly entangled itself.
A military force had been sent to support the attempt of
Ragonath Rao, an exile and pretender to the Mahratta
chiefship, to overturn the actual government at Poona.
Ragoba, as he was usually called, had on his side executed a treaty ceding to the English, among other
places, Bassein and Salsette, which are so close to
Bombay that the present city stands partly on Salsette
Island. The Bombay authorities, being anxious to
strengthen and extend their position on the west coast,
to make their Presidency pay its way by some increase
of revenue, and to obtain political ascendency at Poona,
entered into this very speculative enterprise without
consulting the Governor-General at Calcutta. Such
bargains with political refugees are familiar but almost
always futile devices. The pretender invariably promises

far more than he can perform; he usually loses more
than he gains by the support of foreign arms; and failure
not only ruins his party at home but greatly damages
and discredits his friends abroad.   In this case the
result produced no exception to the rule.   The Company's troops sent to reinstate Ragoba got very roughly
handled on the plains of Arras, where we fought the
first of the long series of battles between the English
and the Mahrattas, almost all of which have been well
and honourably contested, and hardly won by the victors.
We began, as will be seen, by a defeat; for although the
English soldiers and the sepoys advanced bravely upon
the Mahratta guns, they were checked by the sweeping
multitudinous rush of the Mahratta cavalry; a large body
of the enemy got into our rear by declaring that they
were Ragoba's men; there was confusion between
friends and foes, the cry of treachery was raised, and
the whole force fell back in great disorder, losing many
English officers who tried gallantly to rally their men.
It was our first experience of the Mahrattas, and the
sharpest reverse that the Company's arms had as yet
suffered from an Indian adversary.   The expedition
failed totally, and Ragoba came back on our hands in
great discomfiture.   When the Bengal government
received from Bombay a copy of the treaty with
Ragoba, they had written at once peremptorily disallow-
ing it, and declaring the war to be "impolitic, dangerous,
unauthorised, and unjust"; but before their letter
reached Bombay the war had begun, and although after
the fight at Arras the Bombay government could scarcely
maintain that these views, so pointedly enforced by the
Mahratta sabre, were altogether unsound, yet they pleaded

hard against the abandonment of Ragoba and of the lands he had ceded to them. They had taken their payment in advance by occupying Salsette and Bassein, and refused to restore them to the victorious party at Poona.

The whole business was indefensible; but the points occupied were very important, and the Court of Directors sanctioned their retention. Hastings, although he condemned the original enterprise as rash and ill managed, thought that by retreating precipitately and abandoning what we had taken we should only lose more reputation and incur greater danger of a counter-attack; so he proposed that we should hold our ground and face our reverses. In his opinion our honour and interest demanded that we should assume an attitude of this kind as a preliminary means of extricating ourselves decently from an awkward complication. Colonel Upton was accordingly deputed direct from Calcutta to Poona with instructions to endeavour to restore peace on the basis of our retention of Salsette and Bassein; but the reluctance of both sides to give way on this point protracted negotiations up to the end of 1776, and in 1777 matters took a new and alarming turn. The complexion of European affairs evidently portended a fresh outbreak of hostilities between France and England, for which both governments were by this time making preparations. A French adventurer named the Chevalier St. Lubin had induced the French minister to entrust him with a commission to visit India, reconnoitre the situation, and to report on the practicability of landing a force upon the coast from the Isle of France. He arrived at Poona early in 1777, bringing presents and letters to the Mahratta Court from the King of France. The Mahratta

government naturally took this opportunity of requiting
us for our exertions in Ragoba's cause by encouraging
these French overtures, to the alarm and indignation of
the English, who knew that France was about to join
the American colonies against us. As the Mahrattas
within India, and the French outside, were the only powers
of whom Anglo-Indian governments then took serious
account, a combination between them threatened grave
dangers; and the French were now treating with the
Peshwa for a seaport on the Malabar coast that would
be handy for access not only to Poona but to Bombay.
Orders were sent from Calcutta to Bombay to make
certain demands and remonstrances that were calculated
to bring on a fresh rupture with the Poona ministry.
The Bombay Presidency proposed a second expedition
to reinstate Ragoba, who had this time made it absolutely clear to them that he only needed a military escort
up to Poona, where he would be welcomed with accla-
mations; and Hastings, overruling Francis and Wheler,
very imprudently sanctioned it. The news of war
having actually broken out in 1778 between France
and England confirmed and accentuated all the motives
and reasons for attacking the Mahrattas. A force was
despatched under Goddard from Bengal across the whole
breadth of the Indian continent to act with the Bombay
troops; a treaty was made with the ill-starred Ragoba,
as feeble and plausible a pretender as ever ruined his
party and disgraced his backers; and Hastings tried to
detach from the Mahratta federation the powerful Bhonsla
Rajah of Nagpore, known in Parliamentary reports as the
Bouncello. But the Bombay government, anxious to be
first in the field and to monopolise the triumph, pushed

their troops forward on Poona without waiting for the Bengal contingent, and very soon plunged into a morass of troubles. Ragoba's promises and prospects proved equally illusory;[1] the civil and military officers quarrelled, the army was harassed, brought to a standstill, and the invasion was, in short, ignominiously repulsed. When Goddard arrived and took command he restored the credit of our arms; but the war went on until in 1782 it was terminated, after immense expenditure, by a disadvantageous treaty that in no way raised our reputation with the Mahrattas, or diminished their power to annoy us.

It has seemed worth while to give some account of these questionable proceedings, because the Mahratta war may be taken to have been the fountain-head of the deep waters in which Hastings soon afterwards very nearly lost his footing. The Mahrattas soon proved themselves his superiors in Oriental diplomacy, and very awkward antagonists in war. They were a confederacy of notable military chiefs, who, while they were constantly quarrelling among themselves, and parleying with the English in order to alarm each other, in the end always combined to delude and resist the foreigner. They held in the centre of India a position which enabled them to threaten

[1] "We reflect with some concern on the difference between the expectations we were flattered with on our arrival at the top of the Ghâts, and the actual state of affairs. We were given to hope that immediately on the appearance there of the standard of Ragoba, Holkar and many other chiefs of rank and respect would join him with a numerous body of horse. . . . Instead of these respectable partisans, none but a few mercenaries have yet joined us, and Ragoba in a message yesterday gave us explicitly to understand that he had been deceived." (Letter from the civil commissioners attached to the army, 7th January, 1779.)

the three divided English Presidencies, to intrigue successfully against them at Mysore and Hyderabad, and in this way to lay pitfalls into which an incapable governor at Madras or Bombay was very liable to fall. Hastings, on the other hand, was bitterly opposed by Francis in his own Council; his authority was limited and ill supported at home ; the two minor governments, jealous and incompetent, were too distant for effective control ; with these odds against him he was no match for the Mahrattas in a perilous and intricate game of war and politics. He soon found himself overloaded with debt, thwarted and censured in India and England, entangled in hostilities with Hyder Ali as well as with the Mahrattas, and reduced by want of funds to such questionable expedients that his allies and dependents fared rather worse than his enemies. If Hastings had rightly estimated the condition of our affairs in Europe when the war broke out with France in 1778, he would have agreed quickly with his Indian adversaries, instead of striking harder against them ; for with that rupture began a five years' eclipse, the darkest in English history, of the national reputation for political and military capacity. Hastings, who unluckily took the tide of our fortunes at the ebb, was for the time left stranded in India and deserted at home. He saw at once the imminent danger to which all our possessions on the west coast would be exposed if a French fleet, acting in concert with a Mahratta army, should appear off Bombay ; but the emergency only stimulated his energetic temperament to a bolder and speedier stroke at the Mahrattas. "If it be really true," he said in Council,[1]

[1] June, 1778 ; the reference seems to be to Burgoyne's surrender at Saratoga.

H

"that the British arms and influence have suffered so
severe a check in the western world, it is more incumbent
on those who are charged with the interests of Great
Britain in the East, to exert themselves for the retrieval
of the national loss"; and since the instructions from England had left him some latitude in regard to the war, he
enlarged with much vigour the scale of operations. He
soon discovered that his legitimate Indian resources could
provide neither men nor money sufficient for bringing the
Mahrattas to terms; he became entangled in the disastrous
quarrel of the Madras government with Hyder Ali, nor
did he finally extricate himself without some grave calamities and enormous expense. But there is no ground for
Burke's malevolent charge against him that his real
purpose was to pursue unjust and impolitic schemes of
conquest, and to use the pretext of French intervention
to foster his own ambitious desire for aggrandisement, or
that he was guilty of falsehood, fraud, and duplicity.
It is certain that he believed the safety of our Indian
possessions to be in imminent jeopardy, and that by
the force of this conviction he was first impelled into a
hazardous high-handed tone of policy, and next driven
to unjustifiable financial measures for maintaining it.
The dangers were indeed great and manifold enough to
demand the most energetic measures; and to Hastings
they seemed to be closing round his government with
that stormy violence which threatens instant shipwreck,
which sometimes compels a responsible chief to throw
overboard ordinary scruples, and to use all and any means
available for political self-preservation. In this situation
his bold and adventurous tactics in front of numerous
enemies lay him open to the charge of rashness, and

some of his acts are morally inexcusable; yet no lower
motive has ever been brought home to him than an
unflinching determination to preserve at all risks the
immense national interests which he held in charge;
nor can it be denied that under his command the loose
incoherent fabric of the half-built British empire in
India was mainly held together by his energy, and
cemented by his ultimate success. The impending
struggle was long and arduous; but in the end it
cleared the ground decisively.

"I am morally certain," wrote Hastings from India in
1779, "that the resources of this country, in the hands of
a military people and in the disposition of a consistent and
undivided form of government, are both capable of vast
internal improvement, and of raising that power which
possesses them to the dominion of all India (an event
which I may not mention without adding that it is what
I never wish to see); and I believe myself capable of
improving them, and of applying them to the real and
substantial benefit of my own country."

This passage may be fairly taken as embodying the
final purpose and far end which all this rough hewing
of English war and enterprise inevitably tended to shape
out. The gift of political prescience comes from a clear
apprehension of the import and logical sequence of
events; and Hastings saw plainly, as Clive had seen before him, how easily the whole country might be brought
to accept a strong and orderly government, and what
ample elements of moral and material improvement were
contained in its vast population. The thing was to be
done by those who were not to be daunted by immediate
difficulties, or deterred by the novelty of the adventure,

by poverty of imagination, or inability to adapt themselves to unfamiliar circumstances. A story told by
Francis is here so much in point that it is worth insert-
ing. It was written in November 1779 :

"I happened to sup with him (Hastings) not long ago,
when the conversation turned upon Robinson Crusoe. . . .
While the rest of the company were talking, Mr. Hastings
seemed lost in a reverie, in which I little expected that
Robinson Crusoe could be concerned. At last he gravely
declared that he had often read the book with singular satisfaction, but that no passage in it had ever struck him so
much as where the hero is said to have built a monstrous boat
at a distance from the sea, without knowing by what means he
was to convey it to the water. 'And, by Jove,' said Hastings,
'the same thing has happened to myself a hundred times in
my life. I have built the boat without any further consideration, and when difficulties and consequences have been urged
against it, have been too ready to answer them by saying to
myself : Let me finish the boat first, and then, I'll warrant,
I shall find some method to launch it.'"

"This," says Francis, "is the man's political picture
drawn by himself"; and he might have added that the
monstrous boat which our political Crusoe was trying to
launch, with scanty means and difficulties of every kind,
was the British empire in India.

But in 1779 Hastings was like a man who, while he
eagerly surveys a broad road stretching out across the
plain before him, suddenly finds it crossed by a flooded
river in a deep ravine at his feet. "All my political
plans," he wrote in another part of the letter just
quoted, "have been blasted by the precipitate and
miserable enterprise of the Presidency of Bombay"; and
he had a long and exhausting struggle before he emerged
again upon the firm ground in front of him. His duty,

as he regarded it, was to maintain at all costs the
English position in India at a time when the sinews of
the nation were strained to their utmost endurance on
sea and land in all parts of the world. If he had been
well served by able and strong-headed military leaders
like Clive, who had gone, or like Wellesley, who was
soon to come, his policy might have triumphed and his
reputation might have been unchallenged. Men of real
genius have the secret of calling up congenial spirits,
and a good leader is very rarely at a loss for his staff.
But Hastings had no voice in the selection of his colleagues, while in Bombay and Madras, where the fighting
went on, he had little to do with the choice or direction
of his subordinates ; in such a situation the resources of
men and money at his disposal in India were inadequate
for a protracted contest, and many chances of failure
were beyond his control. He was soon reduced to the
predicament of a financier who has embarked upon
some daring and extensive operations, who finds that
his distant agents are mismanaging the business and
squandering the capital, and who must yet either meet
their bills or accept bankruptcy. There is always something picturesque and impressive about fighting battles
and seizing provinces, though the battles may be lost
and annexation be unjust, or even unprofitable ; but
nothing alleviates the blank unpopularity of a desperate fiscal campaign, of empty treasuries, forced loans,
increased taxes, and an administration that is equally
needy and unfortunate. It must always be remembered
that although the long Governor-Generalship of Hastings
intervened between two great periods of annexation, yet
he himself never willingly added a district to the

English territory in India, for Benares and Ghazipur were taken in spite of his remonstrances. He took no provinces and won no victories; he maintained unbroken peace in his own provinces while the Mahrattas were routing the Bombay troops, and Hyder Ali was devastating Madras; so that his strength was wasted and his reputation tarnished in the inglorious business of providing money for carrying on distant, calamitous, and unproductive wars.

CHAPTER IV

HYDER ALI'S INVASION—DUEL WITH FRANCIS

THE full Governor-Generalship of Hastings, as it was established by the Act of 1773, may be divided into two periods of nearly equal length. During the first he was occupied mainly with internal difficulties and intestine broils; he was fighting with his Council or with the Court; driving forward his administrative measures with one hand, and with the other keeping a tight grasp on the reins of his own office. During the second period he was contending against external enemies in the field, or against the troubles at Benares and Lucknow in which he had become entangled by the financial necessities of his foreign wars. In June, 1777, Mr. Elliott, of the Indian service, was passing through Paris on his way to India, when Lord Stormont, our ambassador in France, communicated to him in the strictest confidence the secret intelligence that war with France was imminent, and that the French had formed a plan of attacking the British possessions in India. When this news reached India a French agent was already at Poona negotiating with the Mahratta chiefs, and it appeared to the Governor-General that our possessions on the west coast were in manifest danger. In 1778, therefore, he had pushed a force across India from Bengal to co-operate with the

Bombay expedition against Poona; and he had sent an
agent to the Mahratta chief at Nagpore, with instructions
to offer to support that chief's pretensions to the throne
of the Mahratta State if his alliance could not be had on
lower terms. All these military and diplomatic operations had been more or less unsuccessful, and only involved us for the time in fresh embarrassments. The
Bengal detachment made its way very slowly across India:
the Bombay expedition against Poona failed egregiously
—"they had desperately sent a handful of men against
the strength of the Mahratta empire";[1] and the Nagpore
chief eluded our not very ingenuous proposals to aid him
in obtaining a throne upon which the Bombay government was simultaneously attempting to place Ragoba.
Francis and Wheler, now in a minority at Calcutta,
who had been against any interference in Mahratta
affairs, were confirmed by these failures in their original
opinion, desired to drop the whole business at all
hazards, and hinted that Hastings was continuing the
war to satisfy his own restless and ambitious spirit.
This last insinuation was untrue, for Hastings undoubtedly thought the peril serious, and his temperament led him to meet it by a deep and daring
policy; though he might have done better if he had
peremptorily stamped out the unlucky quarrel which
the Bombay government had begun with the Mahrattas.
But the misfortunes which marred his schemes and
disheartened his Councillors only served to consolidate
the firmness of his purposes. "It has been the will of
God," he said in Council, "to blast my designs by means
which no human prudence could have foreseen, and

---

[1] Grant Duff, ii. 379, 380.

against which I had therefore provided no resource";
yet he was resolved to hold on his course, to send forward fresh reinforcements to Bombay, and to organise
another expedition against the northern possessions of
the Mahrattas beyond the Jumna river. If Hastings had
possessed the full dictatorial authority over all British
India that was wielded by his successors, by Cornwallis
and Wellesley, he might have succeeded in isolating the
contest with the Mahrattas, in avoiding dangerous com-
binations against him, and in concentrating all his available strength against the Poona State in the west. But
war, like fire, is easy to kindle and hard to stop; and
the ruinous military exploits of the Bombay government
were speedily surpassed by the diplomatic blunders per-
petrated at Madras.

Up to the time of the passing of the Act of 1773,
which placed our political relations throughout India
under the control of the Governor-General at Calcutta,
the minor Presidencies had negotiated independently
with neighbouring powers. We had thus become entangled in various contradictory engagements, had concluded offensive and defensive alliances which we could
not keep unless we took both sides in a war between
two of our allies, and had made cross treaties that were
sure to offend one or other of our friends. In 1769, when
we made peace with Hyder Ali of Mysore, he had induced
the Madras government to insert a clause agreeing to
join him if he were attacked; but when the Mahrattas
did attack him we excused ourselves from assisting him
against them. When, therefore, the Mahrattas were
attacked by the Bombay government, they found in
Hyder Ali a willing ally against the English; and thus

the two warlike States that would have naturally fought
each other were united against a common enemy. This
was an ominous confluence of troubled waters; and the
Madras government laid all the blame upon the foolish
meddling of Bombay with the Mahrattas; but it was an
act of their own that opened the floodgates, by stirring
up Hyder Ali and offending the Nizam of Hyderabad.
Acting zealously upon the principle of extirpating French
influence, and showing great impatience of their formal
subordination in external matters to Bengal, the Madras
authorities now contrived to provoke simultaneously
these two formidable neighbours, precisely at the conjuncture when their alliance or at least their neutrality
was most important. The Nizam was closely connected
with the reigning party at Poona, and had declared
against our client Ragoba, but he remained quiet until
the Madras government chose to make a treaty, without
consulting him, with his brother Bazálut Jung, who
agreed to cede us a district. At this he took great
and reasonable umbrage, and threatened to join the
Mahrattas against us. But this was a trivial indiscretion
in comparison with the next false step, whereby the
Madras government succeeded in arousing the smouldering and implacable wrath of Hyder Ali. Upon news of
the rupture with France the English in India attacked
all the French settlements; and although Hyder Ali
warned the Madras authorities that Mahé, a small French
possession on the coast, was under his special protectorate, it was seized by an English force. The only
powers in India whom Hyder Ali respected were the
English and the Mahrattas; and so long as they watched
him on both sides of his country it was not easy for him

to break out; but a fight between his two watchmen gave him an excellent opportunity of paying off old and new scores. He corresponded with the French, who sent him munitions of war from Bourbon Island : he sympathised with the Nizam, who made a league with him ; and in July, 1780, he descended upon the Carnatic with a great and irresistible predatory army, wasting the country far and wide with fire and sword. Colonel Baillie went out against him with a small force, but was defeated and captured ; and the whole Presidency was brought to the verge of total ruin.

Burke's vivid and inflammable imagination was apt to be too inordinately excited by the strange and romantic colouring of Indian scenes and incidents : the sombre tragedy of the Asiatic stage affected him like Shakespeare's rendering of some terrible period in English history; and his delineations of them fall into theatrical extravagances. Yet his splendid description, in the speech on the Arcot debts, of the bursting of this storm upon the plains of the Carnatic, of the havoc and desolation that it caused, of the consternation of the English and the misery of the people, is hardly overcharged. Hastings acted with his usual energy on receiving news of this tremendous calamity. Sir Eyre Coote, who had succeeded Clavering and was now Commander-in-Chief, was sent to Madras with all the men and money that could be collected, and with an order from the Supreme Council suspending the governor of Madras, who was evicted after some controversy, and subsequently dismissed by the indignant Court of Directors. But the mischief had been very effectually done; for Hyder Ali took Arcot and occupied large tracts of country until he was defeated but not driven off by Coote in 1781, after a series of operations which drained the treasuries and nearly exhausted our military resources. The Nizam, Hyder Ali, and the Mahrattas were for some time in combination against us; and their pressure foiled Hastings in his attempt to detach from the confederacy the Mahratta chief of Nagpore, who sent a swarm of cavalry to threaten the eastern frontier of Bengal, and extracted a large sum of money as the price of his neutrality.

The position of Hastings during the year 1780 was evidently one of extreme distress and anxiety. In a letter to the Directors he complains bitterly of "the harsh and unexampled treatment I have received for these six years past in return for a faithful and laborious service of thirty years"; and he alludes to the depression under which he is suffering on that account. "I have now been a second time," he writes, "placed by my king and my country in a post of the first consequence under the British empire, but instead of enjoying that confidence so necessary for the support of this government, I have been treated by the Court of Directors with every mark of indignity and reproach." In another letter (December, 1780) he refers to "the present alarming situation" of the Company's affairs, and reports that "the vast expense for the subsistence and defence" of both Madras and Bombay has reduced him to the "mortifying extremity" of raising loans, has forced him to suspend the commercial investments, and has generally loaded him with heavy financial embarrassments. It must be admitted that at this time our Indian affairs had been so managed as to lower them to the general level of discredit and discomfiture that ruled everywhere

under Lord North's administration. We had set against
ourselves the three principal fighting powers of Central
and Southern India : we had brought down upon our
heads two separate wars on the east and west coasts,
both within convenient distance of French co-operation
with our enemies; and the two incapable governments
that were directly engaged in hostilities depended wholly
for troops, supplies, and competent generals upon the
distant Presidency of Bengal. The Governor-General's
bold and far-reaching schemes had been foiled ; he was
surrounded by enemies abroad, at his wits' end for
money, and thwarted at every step by the opposition
which Francis still kept up in his Council.

It was under the stress of the financial exigencies
produced by this situation that Hastings was driven to
the expedients and exactions which, with considerable
distortion of facts, circumstances, and motives, formed
the substantial ground of the most serious charges in his
subsequent impeachment. But out of the disputes and
difficulties of this period came also another affair, to
which it is first necessary to advert. In North India
Hastings had taken under his protection the Rana of
Gohud, from whom the Mahrattas had wrested the famous
fortress of Gwalior, which was gallantly stormed and
recovered by Major Popham. But Francis had strenuously objected to the Mahratta war generally, and to this
treaty with Gohud in particular ; and although he had
agreed, upon Barwell's departure for Europe, to an
arrangement binding himself generally neither to oppose
the political measures of the Governor-General nor to
interfere with the mode of conducting the Mahratta
war, he contended that this did not apply to the project

of aiding Goddard's operations on the west coast by an attack on Sindia's northern provinces, with the object of diverting the Mahratta forces. He accordingly, with Wheler, disallowed the proposal to reinforce the Company's troops acting in that quarter. This was the particular point upon which the long-standing quarrel between the two men came to a climax; and the understanding upon which Barwell had been allowed to leave broke down with mutual recriminations of equivocation and bad faith; for Barwell's absence gave Francis a majority in Council whenever he chose to thwart the Governor-General, as Wheler voted with Francis and Sir Eyre Coote was absent. Hastings unquestionably believed that he had been tricked, and took his measures characteristically. He conveyed his wife to Chinsurah, at a short distance from Calcutta, and returning alone sent Francis a minute redolent with the bitterness and resentment distilled out of their long personal altercations. "But in truth," he said,

"I do not trust to his promise of candour; convinced that he is incapable of it, and that his sole purpose and wish are to embarrass and defeat every measure which I may undertake, or which may tend even to promote the public interests, if my credit is connected with them. Such has been the tendency and such the manifest spirit of all his actions from the beginning; almost every measure proposed by me has for that reason had his opposition to it. When carried against his opposition, and too far engaged to be withdrawn, yet even then and in every stage of it his labours to overcome it have been unremitted; every disappointment and misfortune have been aggravated by him, and every fabricated tale of armies devoted to famine and to massacre have found their first and most ready way to his office, where it is known they would meet with most welcome reception. To the same design may be attributed the annual computations of declining finances and an exhausted treasury ; computations which, though made in the time of abundance, must verge to wrath[1] at last, from the effect of a discordant government, not a constitutional decay. To the same design shall I attribute the policy of accelerating the boded event, and creating an artificial want, by keeping up a useless hoard of treasure and withholding it from a temporary circulation."

Then came the well-known passage—

" I judge of his public conduct by my experience of his private, which I have found void of truth and honour. This is a severe charge, but temperately and deliberately made."

These words produced the effect intended ; for after the meeting of Council at which the minute was read, Francis drew Hastings aside and read him a written challenge, which was accepted. On the second day following they met at a spot still well remembered in Calcutta tradition, taking ground at a distance of fourteen paces, measured out by Colonel Watson, one of the seconds, who said that Charles Fox and Adams had fought (1779) at that distance ; although Hastings observed that it was a great distance for pistols. The seconds had baked the powder for their respective friends, nevertheless Francis' pistol missed fire. Hastings waited until he had primed again and had missed, when he returned the shot so effectively that Francis was carried home with a ball in his right side. The remarkable coolness of Hastings was noticed ; he objected to the spot first proposed as being overshadowed by trees ; and probably those were right who inferred from his

---

[1] *Sic* in original—? "truth."

behaviour that he intended to hit his man. That the
single English newspaper then published in Calcutta
should have made no mention of so sensational an
incident as the Governor-General's duel, is good evidence
of the kind of censorship then maintained over the
Bengal press. But the editor had recently been in jail
for a smart lampoon upon Hastings and Impey, a
formidable pair of magnates to cut scandalous jokes
upon in those days.

The duel served Hastings well, since it removed the
last and strongest of the three adversaries against whom
he had been contending in Council since 1774. Such a
mode of dealing with political opponents may be thought
questionable ; but governors and high officials of that
period had to be as ready with the pistol as with the
pen, for a challenge was often the resource not only of
irritated rivals but of disappointed subordinates. Fox
had met Adams, and Lord Shelburne, Colonel Fullerton ;
Lord Macartney was called out by General Stuart to
account at twelve paces for some censure which he had
passed on the general during his Madras governorship ;
and Sir John Macpherson, who held the Governor-Generalship for a time after Hastings, met an offended Major
Brown in Hyde Park. Hastings sent Francis a friendly
message, offering to visit him ; but Francis declined any
private intercourse with his adversary, and some months
later he returned to England, where he prosecuted his
feud against Hastings with pertinacious and inveterate
malignity.

Before Francis left he had recorded his vote against
the measure for appointing the Chief-Justice to be
supreme judge and superintendent of all the Company's

civil courts in the provinces. It should be here mentioned that in 1779 the dissensions between the Court
and the Council in Calcutta had risen to the degree of
actual collision between the two authorities ; that in this
quarrel Hastings had made common cause with Francis
against the judges, and that he had consequently broken
off his alliance with Impey, who much lamented this
rupture of their personal friendship and reciprocal understanding upon public affairs. The Governor-General in
Council had published a proclamation authorising disregard of the Court's process, and had supported it by an
armed force. The Court issued warrants for apprehend-
ing the Company's soldiers ; and summonses on a plea of
trespass were served on the Governor-General and his
Councillors, which they refused to obey. Hastings endeavoured to excuse himself privately, hinting to Impey
that he was "impelled by others"; and in May, 1780,
Impey wrote home that he had been sacrificed to the
union between Hastings and Francis. Open war had
been declared, and the two hostile camps were skirmish-
ing actively—employing writs, summonses, acrimonious
letters, proclamations, contradictory orders, arrests,
releases, captures, rules *nisi*, distraints, forcible rescues,
and every other such missile or weapon to be found in
the official arsenals. The Governor-General in Council
accused the judges of arrogating to themselves the
right to review the orders and proceedings of executive
officers, and of the provincial councils which disposed of
the revenue and judicial business in all the districts.
The judges retorted that the government expected to
indulge their subordinates with impunity in mere law-
lessness and licentious oppression. Public opinion in

I

Bengal seems to have supported the government, whose
pretensions were more intelligible to the ordinary mind.
On this side lay also the advantage in the contest, or at
any rate the balance of damage inflicted on the enemy;
for at one time the judges' salaries remained unpaid, and
the Chief-Justice complained that the attorneys of his
Court were lamentably near starvation.

Sir James Stephen has decided that the Court was
on the whole less to blame than the Company's officers;
and he discovers the real offenders in the authors of
the clumsy and ill-drawn Regulating Act of 1773, which
bestowed powers without circumscribing the jurisdictions,
and which purposely left uncertain the supreme jurisdiction, that is to say, the sovereignty of the country.
However this may be, the judges had so roughly
handled the district courts of justice, which were presided over by the revenue officers of the Company, that
Hastings saw the necessity of establishing separate civil
courts; and these courts were soon found to require
proper judicial superintendence. There had for a long
time existed a central court of appeal in civil suits, called
the *Sudder Diwáni Adálat,* whose powers had since 1773
been vested in the Governor-General in Council, but had
never been exercised in any regular manner. Hastings
conceived the luminous idea of transferring these powers,
with a salary of £6000 yearly, to the Chief-Justice; and
six weeks after the duel he announced his project in
Council, stating, what was perfectly true, that the civil
courts urgently needed the supervision and direction of
a trained expert, and adding that he was well aware of
the misunderstandings and invidious misconstruction to
which his choice of the Chief-Justice for so influential an

office would expose him. The office and salary were to
be held during the pleasure of the Governor-General in
Council. The measure was at once politic, practical, and
effective ; it terminated by a master-stroke the conflict
of jurisdictions ; it disarmed and conciliated the Chief-
Justice ; and it undoubtedly placed the country courts,
which had been dispensing a very haphazard and intuitive
kind of justice, for the first time under a person who
could guide and control them upon recognised principles.
Francis dissented from the proposal as illegal and injudicious. He protested that the government were con-
ceding to their enemy all they had been fighting for ;
he probably saw also the important advantage that
Hastings was gaining by this manœuvre, and the strength
that it would add to the Governor-General's position.
Nevertheless the appointment was made ; and Francis
departed for England with a fresh store of accusations
against both Hastings and Impey, which he so used as
to procure Impey's recall by Lord Shelburne's Ministry
on this very charge, and to increase the growing distrust
and uneasiness in Parliament regarding the Governor-
General's proceedings. Impey accepted the salary subject to refund if the arrangement should be disallowed
at home ; and he appears to have undertaken the
duties in an honourable spirit. Any question as to the
morality of this transaction touches Impey rather than
Hastings ; for even if Impey be held guilty of having
compounded his controversy with the government by
accepting a lucrative appointment, yet the plan of
uniting the Chief-Justiceship with the superintendency
of the district courts, taken on its merits, was a good
and practical remedy of existing evils. Impey's appoint-

ment was very soon rescinded, with strong expressions of disapproval; but the principle of placing all the country courts in each Presidency under the appellate jurisdiction of the High Court at the capital is that which has since been adopted throughout India. It must be added that Hastings took the significant precaution, which he may have thought essential, of making both office and salary revocable at the will of the Governor-General, and that this feature of his scheme has not been imitated by modern legislation. For the time, however, the measure answered his purposes admirably; its effect was to soften down at once the bitter conflict of jurisdictions, to reunite the severed friendship of the Chief-Justice and the Governor-General, and to bring back Impey into cordial co-operation with Hastings, whose astute and versatile mind was now revolving projects and expedients of a kind that soon furnished an occasion for utilising his valuable support.

CHAPTER V

THE duel had relieved Hastings of Francis; and he had found a milder method of accommodation with the Chief-Justice; so that he now enjoyed comparative peace in Council and with the Court. But his external difficulties grew and multiplied, to the great detriment of his finances; and there was a constant drain of men and money both to Bombay and Madras. The following extract from a letter written afterwards to the Directors by Sir J. Macpherson while acting as Governor-General, supplies in outline an instructive sketch of the situation:

"Of the general distress of your affairs in all your Presidencies in the latter end of August 1781, when I arrived at Madras, you have long since had authentic accounts; but of the danger to which the very existence of the Company was then exposed, you can have no adequate idea. Your army towards Bombay had been obliged to retreat from a gallant but unsuccessful enterprise towards Poona, and it required great bravery and skill to secure their retreat from the Gauts to the seaside. Your Presidency of Bombay was then near a crore of rupees in debt, notwithstanding the immense supplies from Bengal and their newly-acquired revenues. The utmost of their military exertions, though supported by an army from Bengal, and though they had raised many new battalions, was directed to keep the Mahrattas in check.

"In the Carnatic your principal settlement, and your main

army under Sir Eyre Coote, were surrounded by the army
of Hyder, who had indeed been defeated on July 1st, 1781,
but who from that check seemed only to have become
more guarded and determined in his purpose.   Neither your
army, nor even Fort St. George itself, had at that time above
a few days' provisions in store, nor could there be any prospect of supply from the country.   Your treasury at Fort St.
George was empty ; your credit could not be said to exist in
any active force.   At Bengal, on which your other Presidencies depended almost entirely for supplies, your treasury
was drained, and every effort of raising money by loan, by
annuity, and by partial remittances had been tried, and, to
complete the measure of your difficulties, a rebellion had
broken forth upon your frontiers at Benares, which threatened
destruction to all your possessions from the source to the
mouths of the Ganges, and in every quarter of India.   Such
was the crisis at which it was my destiny to become one of
the members of the superior administration of India.   Few
who could have seen the real difficulties of the part I had to
act, would have envied my situation, and the most obstinate
party contention had but ceased to rage in the scene where I
was to begin my part."

In 1778, on the first intelligence of a French war,
when Hastings looked round him for means of replenishing
his treasury, he had resolved with his Council's approval
that the Rajah of Benares should be one of those from
whom a war subsidy should be demanded in aid of the
extraordinary expenses of the Bengal government.   The
true relations of this personage to the British Government
have been so much misapprehended and so often ignored,
that a short explanation of them, though it has been
frequently given, must here be repeated.   The grandfather of Rajah Cheyt Singh, with whom Hastings had to
deal, was a small landholder who acquired some wealth
and local influence during the troubled period of the
Mogul empire's dissolution, and who obtained the title

of Rajah for his son Bulwunt Singh. When the Vizier
of Oude took possession of the country, Rajah Bulwunt
Singh held under him the lucrative office of farmer and
collector of the revenue in Benares and Ghazipur ; and
when those districts were about to be transferred by
the Vizier to the English, the Rajah wrote offering to hold
them from the Calcutta government on the same terms.
Such independence as Bulwunt Singh managed to obtain
he derived from the protection of the English, who were
interested in strengthening and supporting the possessor
of lands which ran along their north-western frontier,
and interposed between their districts and some very
turbulent neighbours. Accordingly Cheyt Singh, who
succeeded his father, had received from the Vizier of
Oude, through the intervention of Hastings himself, a
formal grant confirming his tenure as zemindar or landholder of the estate which had thus come into the hands
of the family. In those days a man who was strong
enough to establish his authority as collector of the land
revenue on behalf of the State over an unruly tract,
usually found no difficulty in making himself lord of the
land. If he could enforce payment of rents, and maintain
a rough kind of police, his proprietary title as superior
landowner was very soon recognised by common consent.
The tenure upon which the Rajah of Benares held his
estates, and the authority exercised by him over the
people, differed in no essential particular from those of
every considerable landholder who rose to rank and
power in the provinces which gradually fell away from
the imperial government during the eighteenth century.
In such times, as no one heeds the ordinary tax-gatherer,
the provincial governors, who are often busy in making

themselves independent, find themselves obliged to treat,
for the management of turbulent cultivating communities
or groups of distant villages, with some leading man of
local influence who has probably distinguished himself for
contumaciousness and insubordination, and who undertakes to levy rents on his own account, paying a fixed
share to the treasury, maintaining an annual force, and
holding himself generally responsible for some element-
ary forms of order and justice. Under these conditions
a district may easily become a domain, and a domain
may become an independent chiefship if the original
sovereignty entirely disappears. The Benares Rajah was
undoubtedly holding his lands on a mere zemindaree
grant from the Vizier of Oude, who levied heavy fines upon
him, when the territory was ceded by the Vizier to the
Company under a treaty which particularly transferred,
as between the two contracting parties, the sovereignty
over the Benares district to the Company. The English
government settled the amount of the annual revenue, or
share of the rent, to be paid upon the whole estate, and
continued the grant to him upon this and other stipulated
conditions, with a guarantee that the annual demand
should not be increased.

But Hastings held that this did not exempt the
Rajah from the general duty that was inherent in all
tributaries to an Indian sovereign, of furnishing extraordinary aids on extraordinary occasions; and it may
be here observed that in this view Pitt afterwards unhesitatingly concurred. The right, he said, had already
been exercised and acquiesced in, and was indisputably
transferred, with the territory, to the Company. In
all ages and countries, however, and especially in Asia,

such rights depend for their validity on the power to
enforce them. Cheyt Singh was now at that stage in the
development of Oriental jurisdictions when dependence
begins to verge on independence, and when the weakness
or embarrassment of his superiors encourages an able and
ambitious chief or governor to look out for opportunities.
He had indeed become much too strong for the Oude
ruler; he had amassed great wealth; he kept several
fortresses well garrisoned and in good repair; he had a
very respectably disciplined force of all arms; and he
was in correspondence with the Mahrattas and other
neighbouring potentates. Some reciprocal distrust had
been growing up between him and Hastings, whom he
had offended by sending a messenger prematurely to
congratulate Clavering on the news of his temporary
accession to the Governor-Generalship, and by other
indications that he was calculating on a change in that
office. When Hastings made out his list of contributions
to be demanded for the war expenses, he rated the Rajah
of Benares at five lakhs for the first year, which were
paid; but the same demand for 1779 met with great
procrastination; and for the third year Hastings, irritated
by rumours that the Rajah was counting on our embarrassments with the Mahrattas and elsewhere, sent him
peremptory orders to furnish two thousand cavalry. The
number required was afterwards reduced, but the Rajah
sent none; and his restiveness increased in 1781, when he
had certainly heard of Hyder's exploits in the Carnatic.
The ordinary prognostications of the end of English
rule in India were afloat, and Cheyt Singh probably
became more than usually influenced by the profound
conviction of the ephemeral nature of all governments

that prevails in all times throughout India. Whereupon
Hastings pronounced him to be intractable and possibly
treacherous.

"The Rajah's offences were declared by the Governor-
General and his Council to require early punishment, and as
his wealth was great and the Company's exigencies pressing,
it was thought a measure of policy and justice to exact from
him a large pecuniary mulct for their relief." [1]

Upon these plain unvarnished grounds Hastings
resolved to lay upon the Rajah a fine of fifty lakhs
of rupees, and he took Benares on his way to visit
the Vizier at Lucknow, for the purpose of directing
personally the measures necessary for enforcing payment
of the money; having determined before leaving Calcutta
that the Rajah should be removed from his zemindaree
if he refused compliance with the requisition. The
Rajah went to meet him at Buxar, but failed to appease
his displeasure; and at Benares Hastings determined to
place him under restraint, lest he should escape from
the city to his strongholds in the hills and woods which
still cover an immense extent of the neighbouring
country. A letter was addressed to him in which he
was required to give satisfactory explanation of behaviour
that was said to look like disaffection and infidelity.
The reply was such that might have been expected from
the attitudes and circumstances of the two antagonists
thus brought face to face on the brink of a rupture; for
the Rajah was in his own city, surrounded by armed
retainers, while Hastings was in a garden house on
the outskirts of the town, far from his capital, with a

[1] Mr. Wheler's statement of facts, quoted by Hastings in his
Narrative.

slender escort and a weak regiment within call. As the answer was equivocal, the English Governor-General boldly sent his assistant, Mr. Markham, to arrest the Rajah at Shewálah Ghát, where he was residing in a building which may be roughly described as a walled enclosure surrounding a courtyard, with an inner hall and several chambers attached to it in the middle of the yard; its front being on a terrace leading by steps down to the river-side. The Rajah was simply told by the English officer to consider himself under arrest. He submitted quietly, saying that he would obey the Governor-General's orders, but that he was hurt at the indignity of being subjected to confinement; and two companies of sepoys were placed on guard. What followed seems to have been entirely unexpected by Hastings, although it is surprising that he should not have perceived that by arresting the Rajah he had removed and probably turned against himself the only responsible authority capable of controlling the armed and excitable population by whom he was surrounded, and who cared nothing for the ulterior consequences of an insurrection. The city was full of the Rajah's soldiery, while Hastings had only a slender escort with a few scattered detachments of sepoys. In such situations a daring act of authority may sometimes succeed, but the air is apt to be so charged with dangerous electricity that the least friction or shock will produce an explosion which blows to fragments all moral influence and political considerations. The two companies on guard over the Rajah had brought no ammunition, and before it could be sent they had been surrounded by large bands of soldiers from across the river. A company sent to reinforce them

was fired upon, whereupon the courtyard filled suddenly
with armed men, and there was a general rush upon the
sepoys, who with their English officers were massacred
almost to a man. The Rajah escaped in the tumult
through a wicket which opened on the river, let himself
down the steep bank by turbans tied together, crossed
the Ganges, and fled to one of his strongholds. Major
Popham arrived with reinforcements at Shewálah Ghát
only to find the corpses of the party that had been cut
to pieces ; and the English officer who commanded the
rest of his detachment lost two hundred men and his own
life in a rash attempt to storm Ramnagar, a massive
irregular structure on the other side of the river, which
was then, as it is now, the palace and chief residence of
the Benares Rajahs. Repeated warnings were sent to
Hastings that his own quarters would be attacked
that night. As this meant that he and about thirty
Englishmen with him might easily be put to the sword,
Hastings wisely made a rapid though not very orderly
retreat after dark to the fortress of Chunar, about thirty
miles from Benares, which had a small garrison of the
Company's troops. Of the Rajah's overtures for peace
and reconciliation he took no notice whatever, even
while he was surrounded by the insurgent army and
almost in their hands ; he declined offers of assistance
from Oude, and even abstained from drawing men or
money from Lower Bengal, lest the consternation should
spread. From Chunar he issued with great coolness and
promptitude his orders for concentrating various detachments from the nearest stations, for attacking the
Rajah's forts, dispersing insurgents, and bringing all the
Rajah's country under the direct authority of the Com-

pany. The commotion in Benares had disturbed the whole country round; the roads were beset; the armed peasantry and banditti swarmed out to attack outlying posts and troops on the march; communications were cut off; all the postal lines were broken; travellers were robbed and murdered; the banks of the rivers, which were the great highways in those days, were lined with armed men who fired upon and boarded all boats; and the news of a great catastrophe spread rapidly to the Company's stations in the vicinity. Alarming rumours went flying through the bazaars, and authentic information came in only through scouts and disguised messengers. There had set in one of those floods of anarchy and confusion that formerly rose with incredible rapidity in a country where up to 1858 all the peasantry carried arms, and instinctively welcomed a suspension of government as a relief from vexatious tax-gathering and police interference, and as an excellent opportunity for settling local differences and clearing off old scores. Some of the Company's detachments in Oude were very severely handled, and Hastings believed that the rising against the English in this quarter was actively fomented by the Nawab's mother at Fyzabad, the famous Bhow Begum, who highly disapproved of the purposes with which he was going to Lucknow, and would naturally use a promising opportunity of making the journey unpleasant for him. The high governing qualities possessed by Hastings, his calmness in danger, his capacity for collecting and employing vigorously all his available strength, his address and dexterity in handling all the springs of administrative resource, were never more conspicuously exhibited than at this crisis.

From Chunar he carried on his ordinary official work, corresponded with the Vizier of Oude and with Sindia, and directed the operations of his military subordinates, who came to his rescue and executed his orders with the greatest alacrity. The disorderly and disjointed resistance of the Rajah was broken down by a few hardy strokes ; Major Popham, the principal military officer within call, confronted the emergency with remarkable skill and energy, the Rajah's troops were dispersed, his forts were taken by assault, the tumultuous uprising subsided rapidly, the Rajah fled with a large treasure into Bundelcund, his zemindaree estates were declared to be forfeited, and were bestowed on a grandson of Rajah Bulwunt Singh ; from whom they have descended to the present Maharajah of Benares, a very loyal and distinguished nobleman.

It seems clear, upon review of this transaction, and after discarding misrepresentations and making allowance for difficulties, that Hastings must bear the blame of having provoked the insurrection at Benares. Whether he was entitled, by the prerogative that the Company had acquired over the Rajah, and by the practice of his predecessor the Oude Vizier, to demand an extraordinary aid and to impose a heavy fine when it was refused, is not really a material question. Shuja-u-Dowlah exacted from Cheyt Singh a much heavier fine on his succession ; and Hastings merely adopted the financial usage of all Oriental rulers, who are not deterred by the risk of an insurrection whenever they feel themselves strong enough to suppress it. He undoubtedly intended to punish the Rajah's contumacy and to supply the fiscal wants of the Company, by placing Cheyt

Singh between the alternatives of paying an enormous
fine or losing his lands; and in this he followed the
recognised custom of needy Indian potentates. But it
would be a radical error to suppose that an English
government in Asia can be administered on the Asiatic
system; for upon the fact that it consistently follows
a totally different system depends its whole force and
stability; and whenever the English in India descend
to the ordinary level of political morality among Asiatic
potentates, they lose all the advantages of the contrast.
And although in the confused and transitional period
of Hastings' Governor-Generalship these principles were
neither plainly affirmed nor easily acted upon, nevertheless his conduct was at least impolitic and imprudent;
while the rash attempt to arrest the Rajah in the midst
of his own troops can only be explained on the supposi-
tion that Hastings had been too long accustomed to deal
only with the milder-mannered population of Lower
Bengal. There is, moreover, a touch of impolitic severity
and precipitation about his proceedings against Cheyt
Singh, which gives colour to the suspicion, promulgated
by his enemies, that Hastings was actuated by a certain
degree of vindictiveness and private irritation, and had
determined to disable or depose a man who was personally obnoxious as well as obstructive to his policy. On
the other hand, the account given of this affair by
the speakers who prosecuted this charge in the Trial
contains little better than a mere burlesque of the true
facts and circumstances. Mr. Anstruther declared that
the Roman government, even at its most degenerate
period, would not have borne with any proconsul who
should have defended such oppression by a reference to

the practices of Nero and Caligula. And Mr. Burke, after
drawing a picture of the Rajah degraded in the eyes of
his people beyond human consolation by his arrest, and
insulted while he had returned to his closet to address
himself to the Divinity, the Common Father of All,
rejects with scorn the idea that the degradation was less
because Cheyt Singh was not a Brahmin, asking whether
if the Lord Chancellor were arrested while at his devo-
tions the disgrace would be less because he was not a
bishop. The real point of this wonderful parallel lay in
its allusion to Lord Thurlow, who was presiding at the
moment, and whom it would have been exceedingly difficult to disturb at any devotional exercise ; but the passage
is a fair specimen of the astonishing jumble of ideas and
distortion of facts which most of these speeches disclose.

The Benares insurrection had virtually been put down
by the end of September, 1781, and in October Hastings
returned to Benares, where he reorganised the whole
administration of the Rajah's estates. The incident had
no material effect upon his system of foreign relations.
At Chunar he had negotiated and arranged treaties with
the two Mahratta chiefs, Sindia and the Rajah of Berar ;
and he was visited there by the Nawab of Oude, who
offered him a present of ten lakhs of rupees. Hastings
accepted the money, as he himself said, without hesitation, "being entirely destitute both of means and credit
for the public service or the relief of his own necessities";
and he accounted for the money a few months later to
the Company's treasury. But in reporting the matter to
the Court of Directors he suggested for their consideration whether this sum might not be adjudged to him as
a mark of their approbation of his labours ; although he

was aware, as he wrote privately to a friend, that the
letter "would be thought extraordinary ; indiscreet by
his friends and presumptuous by his enemies." The
result fulfilled and even surpassed all these anticipations
so completely that one can only wonder how Hastings
came to write a letter of which he foresaw that every one
would disapprove. The Directors very coldly declined
to present him with the money ; and he soon found
reason to complain of being subjected to much the same
suspicions and reflections as if he had surreptitiously
pocketed the Nawab's gift. His letter to Major Scott,
explaining the grounds upon which he asked for the
money, reads as if he thought he might have been
warranted in making some provision for himself if the
Company's treasury had not at the time been so empty.
He had possibly thought of retaining a part of the sum
until the sanction of the Directors to his doing so should
have been received ; but the whole transaction was in
every respect imprudent. And the bare notion that the
Directors might formally entertain his application to be
reimbursed the sum he had paid into their account, is
one among many proofs that the long absence of Hastings
from England, and his acclimatisation to a different
atmosphere of public life, had obscured his understanding
of the state of feeling at home, or of the temper with
which all the acts and writings of Indian officials are sure
to be scrutinised.

In the meantime he was severely pressed for money
to carry on the war in the Madras and Bombay Presidencies, where the public funds were exhausted, the
revenues in confusion, the pay of the troops in arrear,
and the governments, especially at Madras, in a state of

extreme dejection. The Madras government had written to Bengal (September, 1781) : "We know not in what words to describe our distress for money ; nor can any conception you can form of it exceed the reality"; and from Bombay they received advices in July that no funds remained for keeping troops upon foreign service, that every man was needed for the protection of British territory, that no aid could be spared for Madras, and that the rupture with Holland, combined with the Mahratta war, had reduced the Presidency to a defensive attitude in a position of great jeopardy. The Benares insurrection, in these circumstances, brought his financial embarrassments to their climax ; for disturbances in India always cause a temporary suspension of revenue payments in the districts affected, as no one will pay taxes to a government in trouble. The Nawab of Oude himself owed large arrears of debt to the Company, and had no means of discharging it. When, therefore, he came to discuss the situation with Hastings at Chunar, and was asked to find money for the emergency, the Nawab, while explaining that he had none of his own, pointed out that nothing but the guarantee of the Bengal government itself prevented his laying hands on a reserve that would for the time sufficiently relieve the necessities of both.

The late Nawab, Shuja-u-Dowlah, had left at Fyzabad a large treasure, estimated at two millions sterling. On his death this money was detained by the two Begums, his mother and his widow, who also kept possession of several rich and extensive districts or *jágirs*, which they governed as their appanage quite independently of the Oude sovereign. Shuja-u-Dowlah died heavily in debt; he owed large arrears of subsidy to the Company ; and his son Asaph-u-Dowlah, a weak and ill-guided ruler, made some futile attempts to enforce his claims upon the treasure. In 1775 the widow had been persuaded by the British Resident to pay a certain sum to her son the Nawab, on condition that the Bengal government should guarantee his engagement to demand no more of her; a guarantee that was given by the Council notwithstanding the dissent of the Governor-General. What the Nawab now proposed was that Hastings should untie his hands; should withdraw the guarantee of 1775, and should enable him to replenish his own exchequer and to repay his debts to the Company by seizing the estates of the Begums, who were to be compensated by pensions or suitable allowances. These princesses were ladies of remarkable energy and resolution in politics. They kept on foot large bodies of well-armed men : they had easily set the Nawab at defiance; and the younger Begum had undoubtedly taken care that the Benares insurrection should not die out for want of any fuel that she could add to the conflagration. She had declared that she would throw her cash into the river rather than give it up to her son ; and as a matter of fact the Begums held both treasure and territory by their own strength and the Nawab's weakness, for no Eastern king who had the power would have hesitated about making them contribute largely to his wants. Hastings, who had originally voted against the guarantee, was now convinced that the Begums had fomented the commotion in Benares ; and the pressure on him for money to keep up his fighting line against Hyder Ali and the Mahrattas

was tremendous; so he readily agreed to let the Nawab
have his will with the *jágirs*. If this had been all, it
might have been excusable; for the Nawab's case against
the Begums was a good one, and the British Government
was not bound to stand for ever in his way. The Nawab
was overwhelmed with debt; his troops were mutinous,
and his whole administration out of gear for want of
money; while the Begums and their followers openly set at
nought his authority. But Asaph-u-Dowlah was timid and
irresolute; the Begums were stubborn and indignant; the
Nawab was daunted by their resistance. He applied for
aid to the English Resident, asked for English troops to
oppose the Begums' levies, tried to evade the compact,
and angered Hastings by faint-hearted and dilatory proceedings. Hastings was not in a temper to release his
confederate in a profitable enterprise, or to abandon a
work to which he had set his hand, because the instruments were too pliable. He now pressed not only for
the resumption of the estates but also for the appropriation of the large treasure, or part of it, which the Begums
were known to possess; he insisted on rigorous treatment of the two eunuchs whom he believed to be at the
bottom of all the opposition to his policy, whom he
accused of having stirred up insurrection, and who were
certainly not infirm effeminate guardians of the harem,
but the chief advisers and agents of the Begums, men
of great wealth and influence in the palace, and in command of the armed forces. The Company's troops were
marched to Fyzabad; the palace was blockaded; the
eunuchs arrested and put in irons; and the Governor-
General warned the Resident that he had gone too far
to recede, that he would not endure defeat. "My

conduct," he wrote, "in the late arrangements will be arraigned with all the rancour of disappointment and rapacity, and my reputation and influence will suffer a mortal wound from the failure of them." That he should have determined not to be baffled by resistance, active or passive, is in accordance with his whole character, and if the fixed end lay beyond ordinary means of attainment, he put the blame on those who compelled him to choose between force and failure.

Sir Elijah Impey had left Calcutta to inspect the provincial courts just placed under his charge. On his way up the country he heard of the outbreak at Benares, was pressed by Hastings to join him, and found the Governor-General at Chunar, where he was writing his narrative of the Benares affair and was anxious to have the facts properly authenticated. Impey suggested verification by affidavits; whereupon Hastings proposed that Impey should himself take them at Lucknow, and he availed himself of this excellent opportunity for obtaining the opinion of a Chief-Justice upon the case against the Begums, who were said to have rebelled against their lawful sovereign. Impey ruled that if the Begums were in actual rebellion, it was necessary to the existence of the Nawab's government that he should have the power of taking away the treasures which enabled them to support rebellion. He also agreed to convey this opinion to the Resident at Lucknow, whose known "mildness of temper" might be detrimental to vigorous counsels, should the Nawab prove, as turned out, no match for his mother. Middleton accordingly wrote to Hastings in December, 1782: "Your pleasure respecting the Begums I have learnt from Sir Elijah Impey, and the measures

heretofore proposed will follow the resumption of the
jágirs."   In his examination upon the trial of Hastings
Impey says that a great multitude of affidavits were
sworn before him at Lucknow, of which a few had been
written in English, but that what the natives deponed he
did not know and was not expected to inquire. So the
verification was after all futile enough; it did Hastings
no good and Impey much harm, for an English Chief-
Justice surely travels out of his way when he goes about
a foreign country taking affidavits in support of the
Governor-General's political escapades.   Hastings might
well desire that the evidence which he was collecting to
implicate the Begums in Cheyt Singh's revolt should be
attested "in the most authentic and sacred manner";
nevertheless Impey might have thought twice before
allowing himself to be persuaded into officiating upon
this strange mission, or into giving his legal countenance
to raids upon the Begums' money-bags. And upon a connected review of the relations between Hastings and
Impey it is manifest that they had a general tendency
to bring Impey into trouble; that the profit usually lay
with the Governor-General at the cost of the Chief-
Justice, and that in pulling the chestnuts out of the
fire for Hastings he frequently burned his own fingers.
His good faith and intentions have not been dis-
proved, but he was clearly amenable to the superior
force of character that Hastings could exert on critical
occasions.

Fortified by the affidavits and the advice of the Chief-
Justice, the Resident at Lucknow had put some heart
into the Nawab for his campaign against the Begums,
who treated their sovereign with the utmost contempt

until the English troops came to aid and protect him. The elder lady told the Resident that if he would only stand neutral she would speedily dispose of the Nawab, his prime minister, and his army; but the Resident had very different instructions. The Nawab hesitated to move, not only through fear of the Begum's "uncommonly violent temper," but also from a certain apprehension lest if he encouraged the English to interfere in his domestic affairs, they might prove in the end even more troublesome than his grandmother; but at length he marched to Fyzabad with the British Resident. The Begums, although they mustered a large body of men and threatened battle, did not venture upon resistance; the troops were quietly disarmed or dispersed; the districts in their possession were resumed; the palace was blockaded; the eunuchs surrendered, were imprisoned and forced to give up some secret hoards of money that were in their own houses; and the Resident returned to Lucknow with a sum of money equal to the liquidation of the Nawab's debt to the Company. It should be added that a cash allowance equal to the land revenue of the estates was guaranteed to the Begums by the Company, and that the residue of it is still paid for the maintenance of their heirs and dependents.

So far as the policy of Hastings consisted in spurring on the Nawab to resume the vast estates which the Begums ruled with all the power and revenue of a petty sovereign and no public responsibilities, it was fairly defensible in the interests of both governments. As the Bishop of Rochester put the case afterwards on the trial: "The Nawab owed the Company a large debt; Hastings represented the Nawab's principal creditor; he

compelled the Nawab to reclaim property unjustly withheld and to apply it to the discharge of his debt." But
the methods of duress and compulsion which have given
such a sombre colour to this transaction were used to
extort the treasure. Hastings was at the time in very
serious need and perplexity; England was at war
with America, Spain, France, and Holland, of whom
the last two maritime powers threatened India; and
within India the English were locked in a desperate
struggle with Hyder Ali and the Mahrattas. He believed that all our Indian possessions, for which he was
personally responsible, might be lost if funds could not
be provided for making head against our enemies. It
seemed to him intolerable that in this emergency the
Company should be kept out of money due from Oude,
because the Nawab was too feeble and vacillating to
recover a large reserve of treasure upon which the State
had a very fair claim; and since he held the demand to
be lawful and the necessity urgent, he had no mind to
be foiled by the fidelity of eunuchs or the indignation of
ladies. Nevertheless the employment of personal severi-
ties, under the superintendence of British officers, in
order to extract money from women and eunuchs, is an
ignoble kind of undertaking; and it is impossible not to
adjudge serious blame to Hastings for having taken
a prominent part in such a business. He did not
plainly understand that all such ways and expedients
lie completely outside the range of English political
methods, and that a governing Englishman loses caste
and honour who takes a share, directly or indirectly,
in these sinister fiscal operations. To cancel the guarantee and leave the Nawab to deal with the recalcitrant

princesses was justifiable ; to push him on and actively
assist in measures of coercion against women and eunuchs
was conduct unworthy and indefensible. In this instance,
as in the Rohilla war, and indeed in all joint under-
takings and conventions in India, the finger of public
opinion invariably points to the Englishman as the
responsible partner; and, however modestly he may
remain in the background, his Oriental colleagues usually
take care that he shall find himself in the front of the
prospectus, especially if the business in hand be awkward
and unpopular. The whole odium of the coercion fell upon
the English, for the Nawab took care to give out that he
was their unwilling tool; and although Hastings, while
admitting his determination not to be defeated in a public
trial of strength with the Begums, affirms his ignorance
of the mode in which his orders were carried out, it is
clear that he relied much too confidently on that very
perilous doctrine of the justification of means by their
end. Hastings was himself quite aware that his personal
character would suffer from his conduct; but he said
openly at his trial that he made this sacrifice deliberately
in a great public emergency. To devote one's character
to the cause of one's country is at least patriotic; and
the inflexible grip with which he held the Nawab to the
execution of his contract did expose him to severe
obloquy, and to savage denunciations from the managers
of his impeachment. He was described as one who
had compelled a son to rob his parents; Burke read
passages from a commentary on the Koran by Demetrius
Cantemir, " the prince and priest of Moldavia," to prove
the sanctity of the parental character among Mahommedans ; while Sheridan declared that Hastings forced

a dagger into the Nawab's clenched hand, and pointed
it against the bosom of his mother.

One of the internal reforms effected at this time by
Hastings may be here mentioned, because it laid in some
degree the foundation of the existing Revenue Board in
Bengal, and also led to one of the wildest charges made
against him at the impeachment. In 1781 he abolished
the provincial Revenue Councils and substituted a Committee of Revenue in Calcutta, consisting of four English
officers. The object was to concentrate at headquarters
the chief direction and control of the most important
administrative department, but the details of the land
revenue system were not at that period sufficiently
settled or organised, and the plan seems to have worked
ill by reason of leaving too much to native subordinates,
particularly to a chief agent or Dewan called Gunga
Govind Singh, whom Hastings trusted and promoted.
Moreover, the fact that Hastings kept to himself the
appointment to this committee roused much jealousy,
although an Indian governor of the present day would
probably do the same. At the trial Burke poured out
a vial of his most fervid wrath upon this institution.
He declared that it was a systematic plan of the most
daring bribery and peculation, that Hastings composed
the new committee of his own creatures and favourites,
and that the members were "mere tools to a detestable
instrument of corruption," whom he called Congo Singh.
The evidence given by witnesses at the trial to this
man's character is diverse. Hastings, after his usual
steadfast fashion, stood by him to the last, and on
leaving India recorded a minute attesting Govind

Singh's fidelity, diligence, and ability. He added—
"To myself he has given proof of a constancy and
attachment which neither the fears nor expectations
excited by the prevalence of a very different influence
could shake, and at a time when those qualities were so
dangerous that, far from finding them amongst the
generality of his countrymen I did not invariably meet
with them amongst my own."

This is not the language of a guilty tyrant bidding
farewell to the instrument of his enormities, though it
must be said that Mr. Shore, afterwards Lord Teignmouth, who had been chief of the Revenue Committee,
thought that Govind Singh's behaviour was neither
better nor worse than was to be expected from a native
entrusted with far too much authority, which he probably misused. Burke, however, after declaring this man
to have been the infernal agent and *âme damnée* of the
Governor-General, called him the most atrocious villain
that India ever produced, said that all India turned
pale at his name, and proceeded to give such horrific
descriptions of the diabolical cruelties alleged to have
been practised by him on the ryots—for all of which he
made Hastings responsible—that Mrs. Sheridan fainted,
and Burke himself, while imploring their lordships to
avert Divine indignation from the British empire by
their sentence on Hastings, became greatly agitated, was
taken ill, and obliged to break off abruptly.

CHAPTER VI

END OF THE WARS IN INDIA

"IN these times of calamity and distress," writes the ingenious author of the *Sair ul Matákharin*, "I arrived in Calcutta, where I paid a visit to the Governor-General. That Viceroy, who has a vast fund of innate goodness, condoled much with me, but he was so overwhelmed with public business that he could not give me many hearings." Our native historian found the Calcutta government almost destitute of men and money, and he has recorded some quaint reflections upon the English habit of attributing their misfortunes entirely to material causes, and of relying so exclusively upon the temporal weapon that no room is left for Divine interposition.[1] The tide of affairs was indeed still running against the English in Southern India, though matters had slightly improved while Hastings was occupied at Benares and Lucknow. From both Madras and Bombay had come

[1] "For the English trusted much to the goodness of their troops and to the talents of their commander ; nor do they admit any interference of the Deity in the affairs of this world ; but attribute their repeated victories and numerous conquests to the good conduct of their officers, and to the bravery of their troops ; nor do they ascribe the defeats given to General Carnac and to General Munro to anything else but to the misconduct of those two men, whom they loaded with imprecations and obloquy, as the principal

entreaties that he would make peace with the Mahrattas, but they demanded the restoration of all the places and districts acquired by the English since the first beginning of hostilities, terms which Hastings rejected peremptorily as fatal to British interests and disgraceful to the English name. In March, 1781, a detachment of French troops had landed at Pondicherry, and had effected a junction with the Mysore forces, which were nevertheless severely defeated by Coote at Porto Novo in July. Coote had been invested by the Governor-General with the entire command of all the forces in the Madras Presidency : an arrangement which excited great jealousy and acrimonious disputes, and led to much irritation between Hastings and Lord Macartney, who had taken up the Madras government in 1781. Early in 1782 Hyder Ali's famous son Tippoo managed to surround and cut to pieces a body of English and native troops under Colonel Braithwaite, one of those obscure and forgotten commanders of detachments, whose fortitude and heroism in many a desperate skirmish, or behind some rough entrenchment, are now only remembered by those who read the original reports and despatches of those days. The half-effaced slabs that may still be found below the glacis of the crumbling forts, or in the depths of some jungle, are the stones upon which England has

authors of those disasters that had disgraced their nation. There is no doubt indeed but that wisdom and prudence bear a great sway in the direction of the affairs of the world ; but not so much either, as that the original mover of all events, He that has created and bestowed that wisdom and prudence, should remain idle Himself, and, as it were, out of office, or that the affairs of the world, for want of apparent solidity and permanency, should be wholly and entirely in the power and disposal of human wisdom and foresight."

raised the fair and stately monument of her Indian empire; their names have already passed away as completely as those of the Roman centurions, whose tablets are still exhumed at Cirencester or along Hadrian's wall. Braithwaite, disregarding a friendly warning, allowed himself to be surrounded by Tippoo's army, and had to defend himself with one hundred English soldiers and twelve hundred sepoys, outnumbered by twenty to one. He formed his men into a hollow square, which was only broken by incessant cannonade and charges after a stubborn and savage contest of twenty-six hours; nearly the whole party was cut to pieces, and the English officers were barely saved by the generous interposition of the French officers who served with the Mysore force.

But the war was wearing itself out at last; for hostilities were now slackening in Europe as well as in Asia. Hyder Ali, that ancient and inveterate foe of the English, died undefeated and full of years in December, 1782, and earlier in the same year peace was concluded with the Mahrattas, who had received simultaneous and independent overtures from all three Presidencies; a coincidence which did not strengthen English diplomacy and caused much inter-governmental recrimination. Large retrocessions of territory were made to the Mahrattas, wherein the lion's share went to Sindia, through whose intervention Hastings had negotiated his treaty. It was for the purpose of conciliating this powerful arbitrator that Hastings brought himself to consent to the dismemberment of the possessions of the unlucky Rana of Gohud (now Dholpur), who had been an ally; while the Mahrattas on their side engaged to join the English in compelling Hyder Ali to relinquish

the places he had taken from them.   This latter article
was never acted upon ; for the Mahratta prime minister,
a man of high degree in statecraft, saw that by holding
it in suspense over the belligerents he could keep in his
hands the balance of power between Hyder Ali (or
Tippoo) and Hastings, for both of whom he had too
sincere a respect to desire that either should be prematurely relieved of his antagonist.   And although
Hastings reminded the Mahrattas that if the fanatic
Mahommedan power of Mysore became too strong for
the English, Tippoo would speedily turn and rend his
Hindu rivals and neighbours at Poona, yet even this
argument did not convince the far-seeing Mahratta
statesman that it was safer to strengthen the Englishman.

The treaty was finally ratified in 1783, when Hastings
at last emerged out of the stormy zone of war by which
he had for the last five years been encompassed ; and
also saw some reasonable prospect of attaining, before
the end of his long Governor-Generalship, something of
that unity and concord in his Council which had been so
strenuously and vainly prescribed at the beginning.
Tippoo Sultan had continued the war after his father's
death ; but it ceased when the French withdrew from
him their support on concluding peace with the English
in 1783.   Lord Macartney submitted to terms with
Mysore of which Hastings disapproved, and which he
unsuccessfully tried to amend.   The details of this dis-
agreement are now void of interest, except so far as they
exhibit the extraordinary difficulties that in those days
surrounded a Governor-General who was held, then as
now, responsible for the foreign policy of India, and

whose authority was thwarted and enfeebled by distance, and by the susceptibilities, local prejudices, partial views, and involuntary misunderstandings that so often affect the relations between the supreme and subordinate governments in India. Sir Eyre Coote had been induced to return to the command of the army in Madras, but he died on arrival; the generals who commanded in his place had been worsted by Tippoo, and if the peace had not intervened it is an open question whether Tippoo and his French contingent might not have justified the dictatorial interference of Hastings by capturing Madras and Lord Macartney together. There ensued a general cessation of warfare throughout the three continents of Asia, Europe, and America. For ten years this truce lasted in Europe, until another and much more violent shock of arms raised a conflagration that once more spread to India, where it revived a war in which Tippoo lost life and kingdom, and the power and possessions of the Mahrattas were so effectively shorn that the English predominance in India was thenceforward indisputably consummated.

But for Warren Hastings the war-time was finished. Bombay had been preserved, and Madras saved, as he himself declared, from annihilation; the Carnatic had been rescued from Hyder Ali; the Mahrattas pacified; and the Nizam conciliated. He had run through very narrow and perilous straits; he had faced heavy and damaging responsibilities, had committed errors and suffered reverses; and had barely rounded without shipwreck one or two very awkward points. Nevertheless he had eventually broken through the ring of obstacles and dangerous rivalries by which the British Government

in India had been encircled, and had so planted our
landmarks as to mark out the groundwork of the British
dominion.   It was the deliberate opinion of Sir John
Macpherson (no friend to Hastings), when he looked
back on the general situation of the English in India in
the year 1781, that while the separation of the American
colonies was a blow and a discomfiture from which the
English nation would speedily recover, the loss of our
Indian possessions would have been such a tremendous
commercial and financial calamity, and would have
transferred such immense advantages to the side of the
French, who would have taken our place and succeeded
to all that we gave up, that Great Britain might have
been forced to succumb in the contest she was waging
against her European enemies, and might have fallen
out of the first rank of nations.

"No person," he wrote, "but one who had once seen the
Carnatic in its prosperity, and who afterwards saw it in the
misery in which I beheld it, could conceive the reality of the
general scene of distress which I have described, as within
the possibility of human events.   There I saw men who
supposed themselves, and who literally were, worth princely
fortunes a few years before, absolutely in want of bread.
The whole substance of a great colony, the credit of a mighty
Company and of ally princes, were extinguished by the
sword of desolation.   'You may come on shore,' wrote Lord
Macartney to me the day I came to anchor in the roads,
'but if the gentlemen who are passengers with you come
along with you, they must sleep in the streets.'   And where
was, at that instant, the existence of the India Company?
Only in the revenues of Bengal ; and in Bengal a situation
of affairs similar to that which existed in the Carnatic was
to be greatly apprehended, and had it actually taken place,
I leave it to your own ideas to reflect whether the general
catastrophe which I have represented as possible, was not to

be dreaded as a certain consequence. France looked to such reversion in your fortune, and when you see her armaments prepared upon a scale of force and expense which is the utmost that her faculties can send against India, you cannot be too sensibly awakened to the dangers you have escaped ; nor consider those events as impossible which could alone reimburse your natural enemies, or give them any prospect of future advantage from such extraordinary efforts."

At any rate, all who have studied the condition of England during the later years of Lord North's administration, before Rodney's naval victory in 1782 had turned the scale, will admit that such a catastrophe might well have decided the war against us all over the world to the destruction of our transmarine empire. And few impartial judges will deny to Hastings the chief merit of averting it in India.

But although Hastings had at last succeeded in pacifying or putting down his enemies in India, in England he was exposed to great and growing danger from personal animosities and strong political antipathies. In 1781 Indian affairs began to engage the serious attention of public men, and from that time forward the subject emerged rapidly into prominence. The reports submitted by Mr. Dundas's Committee provided a sort of arsenal whence both parties drew their war material ; until in 1783 India became the battlefield on which the great Parliamentary captains fought the decisive campaign which ended in the defeat and dissolution of the Coalition Ministry, and which drove such statesmen as Fox and Burke into almost lifelong exile from office. The contest and its result affected to an important degree the fortunes of Hastings, whose name takes from 1781 a notable place in the general history of English politics.

The letters written to him by Mr. Pechell, which are quoted in Gleig's *Life*, give a curious account of the causes and influences that induced the leaders of English parties to treat Indian administration, which Hastings was now understood to impersonate, as a point of some tactical importance in the disposition of their forces and the occupation of the ground upon which they confronted each other. In 1781 Lord North, who at that moment thought himself still fairly safe in office, was well inclined to give Hastings his support; the more so because the misfortunes and discomfiture of England in America, the political blundering and the military incapacity, naturally formed a strong contrast against the handling of dangers and difficulties in India. Lord North was no purist in politics: he would probably not have objected to abate something in the article of morality if he could thereby have got better service from his soldiers and civilians; and he might well be inclined to deal tenderly with a Governor-General who, whatever might be his shortcomings, had at least shown no lack of firmness and masterful ability to face troubles. Major Scott, whom Hastings had employed in England as his Parliamentary agent and plenipotentiary, was graciously received by the king; Lord Mansfield and Lord Bathurst, ex-Chancellors, and Lord Thurlow, the Chancellor, were all in his favour. Nevertheless the internal and external discord which pervaded India during 1780-81 had made noise enough to be heard at home; the Mahratta war, the scandals at Madras, the appointment of Impey to preside over the Presidential Courts with a large salary, the awkward stories about Oude at Benares—all these things

had damaged the public reputation of Hastings. Francis
reached England in 1781 with his accusations and evidence amply and skilfully prepared. Burke was a close
friend of Admiral Pigot, then in the Commons, a brother
of the unlucky governor of Madras whose imprisonment Hastings was supposed to have connived at or at
least to have condoned. His kinsman, William Burke,
had been appointed agent with the Tanjore Rajah; had
been treated at Madras with much attention by Lord
Macartney, but had been somewhat neglected by Hastings, although they had been schoolfellows at Westminster. He was now writing home vehement complaints against the behaviour of the Bengal government
toward the Tanjore Rajah, to which Edmund Burke
replied very sympathetically. Sir Thomas Rumbold
also, who had been removed from the Madras Governorship, had applied to Burke for help in clearing himself
and incriminating Hastings; while the alarming news
of Hyder Ali's irruption into the Carnatic had roused
the House of Commons to appoint two select com-
mittees for inquiry into Indian affairs. And although
Lord North passed two Acts continuing the Company's
charter, for a consideration, for three years longer, and
confirming Hastings in the Governor-Generalship, he was
displaced early in 1782 by Lord Rockingham, in whose
ministry Burke's influence predominated. Burke wrote
to William Burke at Madras that the Lord Advocate
(Dundas) "continues in the same happy train of thinking
which your early impressions had formed him to"; and
that Dundas was about to bring forward such resolutions
as would "free that unfortunate prince and harassed
country (Tanjore) from the wicked usurpations of Hast-

ings." Dundas accordingly submitted to the House one
hundred and eleven resolutions gravely reprobating the
whole system of Indian administration, censuring Hastings and Hornby (the Bombay Governor), and recom-
mending the prosecution of Rumbold and Whitehill, the
two ex-Governors of Madras. The Commons resolved
that Hastings and Hornby had "in sundry instances
acted in a manner repugnant to the honour and policy of
this nation, and thereby brought great calamities on India
and enormous expenses on the Company," and declared
it to be the duty of the Directors to recall both of them.

After several animated discussions the Court of
Directors carried by a majority a resolution setting forth
that they, the Directors, had consistently enjoined their
servants in India to abstain from schemes of conquest
and extension of dominion, and had invariably recommended peace, moderation, and good faith ; whereas their
servants had nevertheless pursued a policy of contradictory negotiations, offensive treaties, and unnecessary and
complicated wars ; thereby piling up their debts and
pulling down their reputation. It was manifestly impossible to expect any change from those servants whose
ideas accorded with so ruinous a system, and the Court
therefore determined that it was expedient to remove
Warren Hastings, Esquire, from the office of Governor-
General of Bengal. This was in May, 1782 ; but in
October Lord Rockingham's death saved Hastings from
immediate recall ; and the Court of Proprietors, reassured
by the change of Ministry, carried a motion rescinding the
resolution of their Directors on the ground that it appeared
from incontestable evidence, drawn from the records of
the Company, and supported by the unanimous opinion

of the House of Commons, that the Directors were unjustly laying on Hastings the blame of measures which
they themselves had originally encouraged and adopted.
They held that the Government-General of Bengal was
using every means to produce a general pacification, that
its conduct merited the warmest approbation, and that
the removal of Hastings would be extremely injurious.

The Proprietors were so far right that the resolution
of the Directors must be admitted to have been a shabby
and somewhat hypocritical attempt to disown their share
of responsibility for what had been going on in India,
and to make a scapegoat of Hastings.   But their vote
very properly aroused much indignation in the Commons,
where Dundas pronounced it insolent and dangerous in
principle, and the Ministry exercised their power of pro-
hibiting the Directors from issuing a despatch communicating to India the decision of the Court of Proprietors.
Gleig gives a letter from Hastings to Lord Shelburne,
who succeeded Lord Rockingham as Prime Minister, in
which he endeavours to combat beforehand any unfavourable impressions that might have been produced by the
reports (which he had not seen) of the secret Committee,
and defends his foreign policy.   Hastings particularly
contends, with truth and force, that the Mahratta war
was originally begun by the Directors and by the Bombay
Presidency ; allowing that the prosecution of it, and the
peace, are his own.   Nevertheless Lord Shelburne, who
was too weak to protect Hastings from the formidable
assaults of the leaders in the Commons, tried to compromise matters by arranging for him a retreat that
should save his honour; but Fox, Burke, and Dundas
were now making the Benares case a text for the

most unmeasured invectives against him, and were diligently collecting every kind of evidence in support of their charges. Lord Shelburne would certainly have left Hastings to his fate if he had not himself been abandoned by his party in 1783, when Dundas brought up a bill for reconstructing the government of British India, for inquiring into alleged abuses, and for recalling the Governor-General. His plan was to send out a new Governor-General armed with extended powers and with authority to overrule Council; a change of system long urged by Hastings as essential, and now seen to be so by all parties. But as Dundas had not joined the famous Coalition, the Ministers had no mind to let him bring out and ride the best horse in their stable ; so the bill had to be dropped in order to make way for the introduction, in November, 1783, of Fox's celebrated East India Bill, which was drawn up in consultation with Burke, having been preceded by several speeches in which Burke violently and bitterly censured Hastings. Francis was now furnishing the ammunition by which these incessant volleys were sustained. Lord Macartney, the first governor who had come to India unconnected with the Company's services, had been deeply offended by the interference of the Governor-General in the military and political business of Madras. All his influence at home was therefore thrown in the scale against Hastings ; while with Burke Macartney corresponded in the same vein. And from a letter written by Sir William Jones to Burke (April, 1784), it may be learned that Burke had warned the Chief-Justice that if he heard of him siding with Hastings he would do all in his power to get Jones recalled.

The best and fiercest debaters that ever led the

Commons of England now combined to treat Hastings as the embodiment of all the misgovernment, corruption, heartlessness, and tyrannous usurpation that had been laid to the charge of Anglo-Indian officials; the issue of a desperate political struggle was staked upon accomplishing his overthrow; and while the unpopularity of the Coalition and the king's detestation of his Ministers saved the East India Company, the Governor-General himself was left unprotected. "Loaded for years as he has been," cried Burke, "with the execrations of the natives, with the censures of the Court of Directors, and struck and blasted with the resolutions of this House, he still maintains the most despotic power ever known in India." Such thunderous language, read a hundred years after it was spoken, still strikes the judgment and startles the imagination; nor was it possible that before an audience to whom Hastings was known only by distant rumours, his reputation could resist the shocks of Burke's scorching and fulminating oratory. And when, to quote Fox's bold metaphor, "a bill framed for the happiness of thirty millions of our fellow-creatures was strangled in the very moment of triumph by an infamous string of bed-chamber janissaries," [1] when, that is, the king's personal exertions procured its rejection by the House of Lords, when the

---

[1] Pitt, on the other hand, described Fox's bill as one of the most desperate and alarming attempts at the exercise of tyranny that ever disgraced the annals of this or any other country. And Lord Loughborough, being at the moment a Foxite, said of Pitt's own Indian bill that it merely stole the Company's patronage and put it into the Minister's pocket. In estimating the real weight and import of the epithets showered on Hastings, we have to remember that his accusers were habitually exchanging equally violent abuse of each other.

Company's patronage and possessions escaped annexation, and the Coalition Ministry, dismissed by the Crown
and deserted by the electors, fell to pieces with a crash,
the defeat of his bitter enemies brought no security to
Hastings. On the contrary, it sharpened their animosity
and left him as much exposed as before to the effects
of it. For although imputations of treasonable intrigue,
corruption, servility, of private and public profligacy,
allusions to conspirators who could pull down the throne
and to reptiles who burrowed under it, taunts, threats, and
invectives flew thick and fast between the opposing ranks,
they were used as the legitimate weapons of partisan warfare, and did little real execution. But when two armies
are furiously contesting some point of vantage which is
alternately won and lost, the most dangerous position is
between the lines of crossing fire ; and this was the predicament of Hastings during the memorable political
struggle that went on from 1782 to 1784. Of the three
East India Bills laid before Parliament in those years by
Dundas, Fox, and Pitt successively, the first two disappeared in the clash and confusion of party strife, were
thrown aside in the rout or trampled down by the victors ;
the third was victoriously carried by Pitt in the teeth of
his defeated rivals. The House was filled with sound and
fury, signifying perhaps nothing to the combatants, but
each and every proposal of Indian reform gave the foremost oratorical champions fresh occasion, incentive, and
material for heaping insults and accusations upon the
absent Governor-General. Hastings had been rather
cruelly handled by Fox and his supporters ; he was now
again, in the debate on Pitt's bill, attacked by Burke in
terms of scorn and detestation, as one who had left whole

provinces uninhabited, " and had exterminated the natives throughout the fairest portions of the globe." It may have been necessary for Burke to stimulate the imagination of his hearers, and to appeal to their passions, in order to overcome the unconcern and selfish inattention with which we listen to a narrative of hardships and injuries suffered in a distant continent ; but he himself saw the events and figures of Indian history through a hazy and distorted medium ; and in order to make his pictures popular and impressive he enlarged and discoloured them beyond all natural proportion and verisimilitude. No more remarkable illustration, indeed, can be found of the change in style and habits of thought that has taken place during the last hundred years, than the fact that Burke's extravagant invectives, which he exploded like charges of dynamite against his enemies, should have been thought fair weapons of war against an absent governor, and should not have greatly offended against the standard of moderation, impartiality, and accuracy prevailing in a country like England. It must be admitted that Burke was savagely in earnest, and that the zealous advocacy of Hastings' Parliamentary agent in England, Major Scott, merely added fuel to the fire, by stirring up the wrath of his antagonists and bringing the defence into contempt with the general public. Almost from the hour of his arrival in London, Scott began to worry and weary the public by pamphlets which followed each other in rapid series, and which only provided matter for somewhat indecorous pleasantry to the wits of the day.[1]

---

[1] See *The Rolliad*, for the

> " Reams and reams of tracts that without pain
> Incessant spring from Scott's prolific brain."

No advocate so dangerous to his client could have been found as one who was fluent and prolix, a Forcible-Feeble without point or discretion ; and nothing could be more hopeless than the imparity of Scott's conflict with Dundas who declared that Hastings imprisoned the princes and decimated the people of India, with Fox who denounced him as a State criminal of the first magnitude, or with Burke who cursed him as a scourge of God by whom Bengal had been reduced to a waste and howling desert.

In 1783, when the coalition between Lord North and Fox brought into power the most determined enemies of the Governor-General, the India Bill gave Burke an ample field for dilating upon the iniquities of the Company generally, and Hastings in particular. He collected and summed up their sins into concentrated charges that had all the effect of a converging artillery fire. He undertook to make good three " universal " assertions—First, that from Mount Imaus to Cape Comorin the Company had sold every prince with whom they had come into contact ; secondly, that they had broken every treaty they had made ; and thirdly, that they had ruined every prince or State which put any trust in them. All the chief acts of Hastings' administration were reviewed and condemned in one tremendous indictment ; he was said to have heaped up immense wealth, and his arrogant prosperity was contrasted with the fate of Monson and Clavering, whose days he had shortened, and of Francis, who had returned to England in virtuous despair. But the essential question before the Commons and the country was not so much whether the Company and their officers were guilty of these enormities,

as whether the patronage of India should be the reward
of an unscrupulous coalition at home ; and on this point
the king and his people were against the Ministry.
Fox and Burke were driven out of office, and their
abhorrence of Indian misdeeds, which was a feeling as
sincere as its expression was exaggerated, must have
been accentuated against Hastings by their defeat upon
Indian ground. Thurlow told Major Scott that Hastings
had put an end to the late Ministry as completely as if
he had taken a pistol and shot them through the head
one after another, and he swore Hastings should have a
red ribbon and a peerage. Lord Temple expressed the
highest regard for him, and Lord Mansfield congratu-
lated Scott on the important victory for Hastings ;
another proof, he said, of the wonderful ascendency
of his fortune. That the victors agreed with the
discomfited party in debiting the lost battle to the
score of Hastings was a method of account that left a
heavy balance against him, as he very soon began to
discover. The cautious and limited protection extended
to Hastings by Pitt in 1784, when he refused to comply
with Burke's demand for papers regarding Oude, only
served to encourage his assailants, and their exasperation naturally increased when Pitt brought in his own
India Bill, which took out of their sails the wind on
which they had relied for a prosperous voyage. To
Pitt, with a strong majority at his back, it was a thing
of small consequence that Burke should threaten the
Ministers with retribution from an offended Deity, as
accomplices in the guilt of deluging India with blood ;
but to Hastings, who had no such practical means of
defying the lightning, and who was soon to stand bare-

headed under the thunderstorm, it was a serious matter that all these vows of vengeance should gradually become diverted and concentrated upon him personally. Yet Hastings had been so often menaced with public ruin and private disgrace, his recall had been so often averted by accident, usually by some turn of the political kaleidoscope;[1] he had, like all who have lived long beyond the atmosphere of English politics, so imperfect a comprehension of the signs of the times, that he necessarily miscalculated his situation and mismanaged his measures for self-defence. He felt distress, vexation, and resentment; he had asked the Directors, in March, 1783, to send out a successor, and he had said that he would throw up office at once if Cheyt Singh were restored to the Benares zemindarship. But he does not seem to have been fully aware that the Coalition Ministry would have saved him the trouble of resigning, for if their India Bill had passed he would have been instantly recalled on the charge of peculation; and latterly he placed faith in the assurances of Major Scott, who relied upon the favour of the king, upon Pitt, Dundas, and Temple, whose support Scott fancied he had secured; and upon Thurlow, who hounded on Scott like a terrier to worry Fox, vowing that he had seen the greatest orators in the Commons struck dumb by a fact. Scott discovered, too late, the inutility of attempting to mop up with "a few plain facts" the surging and foaming tide that was to rise against Hastings; but manifestly Hastings him-

---

[1] In 1776, by Clavering's death, when he retracted his resignation; in July, 1782, by Lord Rockingham's death; in October, 1782, by a vote of the Proprietors; in 1783, by Lord Shelburne's retirement from office; in December, 1783, by the overthrow of the Coalition.

self had at this time no notion that his greatest perils
and severest conflicts were not behind but before him ;
and though he may have felt keen anxiety he had not
the presentiment with which a man looks forward to an
obscure and ominous future—

> " As if calamity had but begun ;
> As if the vanward clouds of evil days
> Had spent their malice, and the sullen rear
> Was with its storied thunder labouring up."

CHAPTER VII

DURING the year 1785 Hastings was still occupied and harassed by external complications, internal dissensions, and chiefly by anxiety about his position at home. At the end of 1782 the resolution of the House of Commons for his dismissal was known in India, and had materially diminished his authority in his own Council, besides affecting his influence abroad. To Lord Shelburne, who had sent him verbally some professions of esteem, he wrote a long letter protesting against the conclusions of the secret Committee. Whether this letter was actually sent is not clear; but it is a remarkably vigorous and pointed composition, full of the strenuous pertinacity and upstanding disdainful combativeness with which Hastings usually rejected censure or challenged an adverse sentence. "I have seen the resolutions," he wrote, "but not the reports on which they are founded. I can, however, boldly venture to assure your Lordship that either the reports must have been garbled, or they are the most positive and direct evidences of the opposite of every resolution which professes to be formed upon them, and which contains my condemnation. . . . I have never in a single instance broken the faith of a treaty, or deserted or injured the interests of the Company. I

have never sacrificed the honour of my nation. I had no
more concern in the origin and commencement of the
Mahratta war than the Lord Advocate of Scotland. . . .
I have been the instrument of saving one Presidency
from infamy and both from annihilation." Hastings
was certainly not one of those men who allow enterprises
of great pith and moment to fail through doubts, mis-
givings, or

> " Some craven scruple
> Of looking too precisely on the event."

On the contrary, he is to be classed with those who,
having said "This thing's to do," and having justified to
themselves their own actions, are only rendered impatient
by the criticism of others, and whose self-approval is not
even shaken by failure.   But his Councillors at Calcutta
naturally took a different view; they were now men inferior in capacity and reputation to his former antagonists;
yet although their opposition was proportionately less
formidable, the minutes of proceedings show two out of
his three colleagues constantly voting against him; while
the third, Wheler, gave him very intermittent support.
In one letter he writes of cavils and contradictions made
in a tone of insolence which often threw him off the
guard of his prudence: "For indeed I have not the
collected firmness of mind which I once possessed, and
which gave me such a superiority in my contests with
Clavering and his associates."

After the Parliamentary censures came the reprimands
from the Court of Directors. In February, 1783, he
received from the Court resolutions entirely disapproving
his conduct in the Benares affair as improper, unwarrantable, and highly impolitic. He evidently perused these

documents with profound indignation and contempt;
and he consoles himself by remembering that his own
narrative of events at Benares, which must have reached
England soon after the passing of these resolutions,
"must have completely defeated them, for if there
ever was a demonstration produced by argument, I have
demonstrated the falsehood of Cheyt Singh's pretensions to independency." He at once set himself to
contradict and refute all that the Court had affirmed.
In a long and peremptory letter he most solemnly and
categorically denied the existence of their facts and the
justice of their conclusions; he declared that if Cheyt
Singh were reinstated at Benares he would instantly
resign; he enlarged on his services to the Company,
and on the patience and temper with which he had
submitted to all the indignities that had been heaped
upon him during eleven years of administration; and he
upbraided his masters for their scurvy treatment of him
in the midst of public dangers.

"While your existence was threatened by wars with the
most formidable powers of Europe, and while you confessedly
owed its preservation to the seasonable and vigorous exertions
of this government, you chose that season to annihilate its
constitutional powers. You annihilated the influence of its
executive member. You proclaimed its annihilation. You
virtually called on his associates to withdraw their support
from him, and they have withdrawn it; but you have substituted no other instrument of rule in his stead, unless you
suppose it may exist and can be effectually exercised in the
body of your Council at large, possessing no power of motion
but an inert submission to the letter of your command, which
has never yet been applied to the establishment of any
original plan or system of measures, and seldom felt but in
instances of personal favour or personal displeasure."

M

These hard-hitting sentences follow each other like the blows of a flail, and must have fluttered the pigeon-holes in Leadenhall Street. He ended by assuring the honourable Court that he was only detained in their service by fear of public damage from his abruptly quitting it, and desiring them to be pleased to obtain the early nomination of some person to succeed him. The Court rejoined by rebuking their Governor-General for unjustifiable animadversions on the conduct of his superiors; but as they did not at the moment desire to drive him to resignation, their letter ended with expressions of great approbation of the vigour which he had shown in the defence of Southern India, and with some admission of the exigencies which had made unavoidable the rather humiliating treaty which he had finally concluded with the Mahrattas.

The Court, however, admonished him on the subject of his treatment of the Begums in language which he thought harsh and insolent, and which encouraged his refractory Councillors, "who," he writes, "all oppose me." "I will resign this thankless office on the first opportunity, but I will not be driven from it either by the folly of my subordinates or the injustice of my superiors." In short, they were all utterly wrong-headed and obstructive, and he was determined that they should not ruin the country and disgrace themselves by driving him out of the Governor-Generalship. It was his nature to dispute with his enemies every foot of ground; his innate fortitude reposed upon a sincere conviction of his own superiority; he was usually right, but when he was wrong he never seems to have admitted it, and his clear intelligence saw its objects so distinctly that he scarcely comprehended hesitation about making straight for them.

The dissension over the negotiations for peace with Tippoo Sultan had now culminated into something like an open quarrel with the Madras government; for Lord Macartney had so persistently withheld obedience to orders from Bengal that his removal for insubordination was discussed in the Governor-General's secret committee at Calcutta. At Benares there had been mismanagement of the revenue, and much discontent on the part of the new Rajah; while at Lucknow the Nawab and his minister were complaining to Hastings that the English Resident was usurping all their authority. For the affairs of the Benares estates and of Oude Hastings felt himself peculiarly responsible; and he was none the less ready to look into grievances because the officials at Benares and Lucknow were men whom he had removed, who had been reappointed against his will by the Court of Directors, and whom he believed to be now thwarting his arrangements, and calculating upon his early departure from India in a manner that he was not likely to overlook. He had thus various matters to settle, and sundry enemies to demolish, before he could wind up his Indian affairs satisfactorily.

Yet the end of his Indian career was manifestly drawing near; he had been thirteen years in chief command; he had outlived or outlasted all his colleagues; and many indications pointed to the expediency of withdrawing before his enemies, whom he had so long resisted, should prevail against him in England and India. His constitution was much damaged; and his wife, from whom he could scarcely bear to part, was so

ill as to be obliged to leave India without further delay.
Nevertheless he determined not to depart until the
Directors should have answered the letter in which he
tendered his resignation, or before the arrival of his
successor; for he had a strong repugnance, not unusual
in similar circumstances, to allowing his discontented
colleagues the chance of taking temporary command; and
upon these reasons he resolved to hold on, if necessary, for another year. "No consideration upon earth,"
he wrote, "shall induce or compel me to act longer with
such associates" as his Councillors, with all of whom
he had now become thoroughly disgusted. Clavering's
open enmity seemed now to him to have been less
disagreeable than the underhand obstructiveness of
Macpherson and Stables, who had come out to India
as his "dear friends"; but in truth it would have
puzzled any set of Councillors to hit off the precise
degree and kind of opposition that Hastings was disposed to tolerate.

So Mrs. Hastings sailed alone for England in January,
1784. Her departure was to Hastings a severe affliction.
He was miserable at losing her; and his first letters to
her after the separation still touch the reader with a
magnetic sympathy for the throb of grief with which he
gazed after the vanishing ship, as it stood out into the
open sea from the estuary of the river. For some days
afterward he seems to have been completely dejected
and unnerved. On the next day he writes to her—"I
followed your ship with my eyes until I could no longer
see it, and I passed a most wretched day with my heart
swol'n with affliction and my head raging with pain. . . .
I am certain that no time nor habit will remove the

pressure of your image from my heart, nor from my
spirits; nor would I remove it if I could, though it will
prove a perpetual torment to me. . . . Oh God, what a
change was effected in my existence within the space
of a few minutes, when I passed from the ship to the
pinnace." And throughout the numerous letters that
he wrote to his wife, until he rejoined her in England, he
recurs constantly to his misery at her absence, to his
anxiety for her health, and to the longing thought of
seeing her again by which he is unceasingly possessed.
He had evidently been accustomed to make her the
confidante of all his official troubles—

"I go to Oude," he wrote to her, "on a bold adventure,
from a divided and hostile Council, to a scene of difficulties
unsurmountable but by very powerful exertions; to a country
wasted by famine and threatened by an invading enemy;
to a government loosened by twelve months' distraction, its
wealth exhausted, and its revenue dissipated. I go without
a fixed idea of the instruments which I am to employ or the
materials on which I am to act, with great expectations
entertained by others but very moderate of my own ; my
superiors at home labouring to thwart and if they can to
remove me ; and all this as well known to the Indian world
as to our own. Add to the foregoing a mind unequal to its
former strength and a constitution very much impaired."

The allusion here is to the project of a final visit to
Benares and Lucknow, upon which Hastings was the
more steadily bent because his colleagues had raised
objections to it. He had indeed some trouble in extracting an assent from the Council, one of whom "wickedly
insinuated" that it was hardly worth while for the
Governor-General to go so far from headquarters when
orders dismissing him from his office were expected, and

might arrive any day from England. The remark, though unpleasant, had sufficient truth in it to make him set out speedily. He left Calcutta in February and did not return until November; so that this expedition practically occupied his last year in office, for he passed the intervening months at Benares and Lucknow.

The state of affairs in Oude undoubtedly called for the Governor-General's presence and personal supervision. Mr. Bristow, who was then Resident at that Court, had been appointed to the post by orders direct from England. Against these orders Hastings had vehemently protested, had been sharply overruled, and had recorded in the minutes that the step was "a most pernicious degradation of the executive authority at the very crisis when the government was surrounded by foreign wars and complications." To which Francis, for whom the appointment was a triumph, had rejoined by minuting that he "foresaw many more dangers and mischiefs to the government from contracting a habit of disobeying the Company's orders," as Hastings was quite ready to do if he could have got any support from his Council. However, it so happened that Middleton, for whom Hastings had originally turned out Bristow, subsequently incurred his chief's displeasure for lack of vigour in clearing off the balances due from Oude, and also in pressing on certain urgently-needed reforms of the administration. The Nawab had neither paid his debts to the Company nor had set his kingdom in order; and Hastings taxed both the Resident and the Nawab's prime minister with culpable negligence in allowing misrule and insolvency to continue. Middleton's resig-

nation gave Hastings an opportunity of appointing
Bristow with a good grace, in anticipation of reiterated
orders to do so; but affairs in Oude did not mend, for
in October, 1783, the country was, according to Hastings,
in universal revolt; so before starting from Calcutta he
persuaded the Council to turn out Bristow.

It must be admitted that Mr. Bristow's conduct had
gone some way toward fulfilling the dire prognostications that Hastings had recorded of the consequences
of appointing him; nor could any good be expected from
sending to the most important diplomatic post in India
an agent notoriously at variance with his principal, who
relied upon the surreptitious support of the malcontent
Councillors for holding his own against so masterful a
Governor-General. The correspondence of 1783 shows
that the Resident's behaviour was a prolific source of
dissension in Council. Hastings thought he "had
secured Bristow's fidelity by his gratitude," but he soon
found himself obliged to lay before his Council charges
sent in by the Nawab against the Resident. The
Board promptly acquitted him on all charges, and
Hastings immediately adjudged him guilty on every one
of them. He reports this to Major Scott, adding rather
naïvely, "You will wonder that all my Council should
oppose me. *So do I!*" But he explains that Macpherson
and Stables had intimidated Wheler, of whose conduct
he is ashamed, and who himself became ashamed of it
later, when Hastings had succeeded by great pains, and
perhaps some little counter-intimidation, in working
Wheler's head round again into the right direction. The
Council was so constructed that its weakest and most
irresolute member usually found himself holding the

casting vote between two fiercely contending factions, and the strongest of them dragged him over to their side. Wheler feebly tried to do his duty, and was rewarded by a sentence in one of Burke's philippics against Hastings, where he stands as "his supple, worn-down, beaten, cowed, and, I am afraid, bribed colleague, Mr. Wheler."

After this fashion the Governor-General and his Councillors had mutually checked and counteracted each other in Calcutta, with the result that for some time Mr. Bristow appears to have attained emancipation from any superior control; he disregarded the instructions given him by Hastings, demurred to his authority, quarrelled with the ministers of the Nawab, treated the Nawab himself as a cipher, and so managed his powers of interference as to dislocate and paralyse a feeble and ill-constructed government. His success in overawing the palace and checkmating the ministers had been so complete that while he was supreme at the capital the provinces were left with no administration at all, and the normal confusion soon thickened into serious disorder. When the Nawab complained of the Resident's inordinate arrogance and of his intolerable meddling in all departments under pretext of reform and guidance, Mr. Bristow alleged that he had received the Governor-General's strict injunctions to insist on the proper liquidation of the Company's claims, and that he was merely acting up to orders. This aspect of the case was of course supremely irritating to Hastings, who recorded a long and exhaustive minute on the Resident's misdeeds, treating him as the instrument and impersonation of the policy that had been originally forced upon

his government by Clavering and Francis, and that had
caused, he said, great and irreparable mischief to Oude.
In this State paper he argues with great cogency that
the disorder and impoverishment of Oude were attributable to the system, introduced against his consistent
protest, of weakening the kingdom and interfering with
the administration; nor can any one read his minute
without admitting that his ideas were at any rate
moderate, logical, and formed upon a connected and well-
considered plan. His policy from the beginning had
been to strengthen the ruler of Oude as our chief ally,
and as our bulwark against other active powers; it was
with these objects that he had engaged in the Rohilla
war, had opposed the treaty which deprived the Nawab
of Benares, and had urged the Nawab to seize the lands
and treasure detained by the Begums. Some of these
transactions must be gravely condemned, but it should
be understood that they were all politically coherent
and founded on the intelligible principle of strengthening those from whom support is expected. It was the
policy of those by whom Hastings had been overruled,
and who laid at his door consequences for which they
themselves, especially Francis, were responsible, that
really brought Oude, as a State, to the verge of ruin: a
vacillating policy of intrigue and intermittent exactions,
of draining the resources of a country and damaging its
ruler's credit at a time when they were both subjected
to extraordinary pressure. With the Nawab of Oude
personally Hastings was always on terms of friendship
and confidence; nor will the impartial student of Anglo-
Indian history find in his acts and language the imperi-
ous, high-handed coercion that subsequently characterised

Lord Wellesley's dealings with the successor of Asaph-u-Dowlah. But Lord Wellesley governed India as the representative of a powerful war-ministry in England at a time when the upsetting of thrones and the levying of heavy contributions upon subject nations prevailed in Europe to an extent which left the English people little leisure to inquire into the grievances of a distant Asiatic principality. It was a period of tumultuous confusion, sudden invasions, and unscrupulous annexations all over the civilised world ; nor can we doubt that Lord Wellesley's proceedings in India took their colour and their justification from the violent struggles for and against territorial aggrandisement in which England and other nations had engaged at home.[1] If Hastings had returned ten years later than he did—in 1795 instead of 1785—no one, not even Burke, would have proposed his impeachment.

Hastings went first to Benares, whence he sent to the Council a long letter describing the condition of that province, which had suffered much from drought, but more, he said, from mismanagement and the oppressive conduct of the chief native officials, who abused their position as the agents of an incompetent Rajah. The particular nature of the tenure upon which the

---

[1] Mr. Spencer Walpole, referring (in his *History of England*) to Wellesley's dealings with Oude, says : " If these occurrences had taken place in Europe, if some Napoleon, for instance, had treated Spain as Wellesley treated Oude, history would have condemned his conduct. But historians apply one code of morality to India and another to Euorpe." But Napoleon did treat Spain with extreme treachery and violence ; and his political crimes were immeasurably greater than any that have been committed by the English in India.

Rajah of Benares held, and still holds, his estates is not
easily explainable to English readers, but it will suffice
to mention here that he is a great landholder, bound to
pay a fixed lump sum to the government out of the
rents of his lands, and that the occupancy or proprietary
rights of the tenants had to be maintained against the
Rajah's encroachment.   The duty of the government,
therefore, was not only to enforce payment of the sum
due to its treasury, but also to protect the inferior
holders from extortion or eviction by the Rajah's land-
agents; and it was toward this latter point that the
inquiries and exertions of Hastings were chiefly directed.
He submitted to the Calcutta Council an elaborate plan
for reforming the administration, removing incapable
officials, and placing under proper regulation the collection of rents and the adjudication of the rights and
tenures.   His proposals were approved by the Council
after due deliberation, upon an understanding that
nothing would be done to diminish the Company's
revenue, and that Hastings would take all responsibility
for changes.   From Benares Hastings went on to Lucknow, where he stayed from March until the end of
August, occupied in aiding the ministers to bring their
government into some orderly shape by regulating accounts, by the assignment of revenue to liabilities, by
the formation of a regular military establishment; and,
above all, by placing under close restrictions the power of
the Company's representative to interfere in the internal
affairs of the country.   He was well aware that irregular
interference with Oriental States, when it diminishes the
personal dignity of the ruler and disarms his authority,
does much more harm than it can possibly prevent.   This

consequence, he said, it had been his invariable study
in his relations with Oude to avoid, by the removal or
restriction of any British influence that interfered with
the Nawab's government.   One of his last acts was to
arrange for the withdrawal of a large and costly detachment of the Company's troops that was stationed at the
Nawab's expense upon the northern border of Oude,
but to this the Council refused, out of regard for the
Company's finances, to accord their consent.   In the
art of administrative organisation Hastings always displayed skill and knowledge to a degree that places him
far above all his predecessors and contemporaries in
India, who indeed (except Clive) were for the most
part remarkably deficient in the higher qualifications
for the political settlement of a great country.   We
may therefore fairly regard Hastings as the founder
of the school of administration that has since had a
not unsuccessful development in India; and as the
ancestor by official filiation of a long line of not unworthy descendants, who have carried his traditions
and continued his methods of revenue management and
orderly internal reformation throughout the provinces
that have from time to time been added to his original
Presidency of Bengal.

While Hastings was at Lucknow, the eldest son of
the Mogul emperor, who had escaped in disguise from
Delhi, where his father was an abject puppet in the
hands of some military adventurers, arrived there and
prayed the English governor for assistance.   The story
of his flight from Delhi, which he wrote, is still extant.
It tells how he let himself down the city walls one cloudy
night, and wandered about the fields in the dark till he

found a peasant watching crops who showed him a ford
of the Jumna, and whom he resolved, after this service, to
kill, "lest he should inform the enemy of my route";
how he spared the man at the last moment on reflection,
and was safely escorted by the friendly folk of the
country—with other details that give a faint glimpse and
reminiscence of old India, such as living Englishmen have
seen and known. The idea of lending a hand to set up
again the great Mogul was not uncongenial to Hastings'
temperament. He proposed to his Council a project of
rescuing the emperor from his distress and durance, on
the grounds of our former connexion with and obligations to the house of Timur, and the impolicy of per-
mitting it to be extinguished so utterly as to leave a
vacuum that might be filled up by a new and much
stronger power. If Hastings had been, like all the other
rulers of that time in India, an independent chief, he
might have struck in at that moment on the side of the
imperial authority with great opportuneness and effect;
he would certainly have driven off the jackals that were
tearing at the moribund carcass of empire; and he would
have found no competitors to dispute with him the
mastery of North India up to the line of the Jumna
river. But the Mogul empire had sunk past the possibility
of revival; he would have found the whole country upon
his hands; and, in fact, he would have anticipated
prematurely by twenty years the exploits of Lord Lake
and Lord Wellesley. And as he was only a Company's
Governor-General, in a most precarious position personally, at odds with his Council, powerfully assailed at
home, accused of rash adventures and unwarrantable
wars, such a proposal, made on the eve of his retirement

from office, stands on record merely as a notable illustration of the hardy and self-reliant spirit of political enterprise that is so strongly diffused through his whole career and character. Left to himself he would probably have succeeded ; for he must undoubtedly rank with that class of men who, if they can find an environment favourable to the unlimited employ of their faculties and resources, are sure to clear a wide space round them in a confused world, make a great splash in troubled waters, and often start a new epoch in the almanac of a country's history.

But the Council refused, very rightly, any kind of countenance to expeditions in aid of the Great Mogul ; and Hastings abandoned the notion without in the least giving up his conviction of its unquestionable expediency. He returned to Benares in August, 1784, during the height of the periodical rains ; his boat was wrecked in a storm on the Ganges, so he travelled by land to Mirzapur and thence by river again to Chunar, where he received by his letters from England news announcing the complete overthrow of his enemies the Whigs. Pitt had dissolved Parliament : the Coalition party had been utterly routed at the elections ; and Major Scott assured Hastings that it was generally wished he should remain another year in India ; that people were, in fact, greatly alarmed at the prospect of his throwing up the government. According to Scott, the Lord Chancellor Thurlow had spoken publicly and privately very warmly in favour of Hastings, and had pressed Pitt to give him an English peerage, declaring, as he told Scott, that Hastings had made him a Minister, and had made Pitt one too ; a

declaration that was probably very unpalatable to the
haughty Premier. Burke had been crushed by one
of Scott's speeches : both he and Francis had been
made completely ridiculous; and Mrs. Hastings had
had a very honourable and gracious reception from
their Majesties. Hastings replied that he was pledged
to resign, and that he was determined to leave in
January, 1785. Nevertheless he seems to have contemplated, on Scott's information, the possibility of
Pitt's Cabinet asking him to continue in office with extended powers, such as are vested in a modern Governor-
General, to overrule his Council and act for himself in
affairs of sufficient urgency or magnitude. He observed
that a proper and dignified pretext for postponing his
departure could only be furnished by the receipt of
orders and instructions of this nature ; and in that event
he said, " I should deem myself bound against every
consideration of domestic comfort, of life, and of fortune
to remain." In short, he evidently desired to try what
might be done in India by a Governor-General who should
be irresistible at the Indian Council-board, and powerfully backed in the British Parliament : the exact position
of his successors, Cornwallis and Wellesley, who used it
to subdue or annex an immense territory.

But Pitt had throughout replied with much caution
and reserve to all these eager demonstrations on behalf of
Hastings ; he allowed him great merit, nevertheless there
were charges against him which required explanation.
Up to November, 1784, he remained in suspense, being
still ready to stay, if required to do so officially and with
extended powers; until any expectations he may have
formed of remaining on such terms entirely disappeared

when accounts reached Calcutta of the debates, especially of Pitt's introductory speech, on the new India Bill. Hastings had written a long letter to Pitt, as to a friendly official chief, expounding his policy, and apparently dilating upon his project of assisting the Delhi emperor. He was therefore confounded and taken aback by the stress and earnestness with which Pitt spoke of the necessity for curbing the ambitious spirit of conquest in the Bengal government, which had cost so much blood and money, of severely punishing disobedience of orders, and of guarding against the continuance of offences that were shocking to the feelings of humanity and disgraceful to the national character, by establishing a special tribunal for the trial of Indian delinquents. The speech, he complained, contained "the same abuse of the Company's servants, expressed in the same trite epithets"; and he learnt with astonishment that Major Scott himself had voted for the Bill. In point of fact, Pitt was so far from intending to support Hastings that he was preparing to issue orders for his recall; having been constantly rallied by the Opposition on his deference to the Company and his alleged tenderness for Bengal; nor did he or Dundas make any answer to the onslaughts of Burke and Fox against the Governor-General. When, therefore, at the end of December Hastings had received and read carefully a copy of the Bill, he treated it as "so unequivocal a demonstration that my resignation of the service is accepted and desired, that I shall lose no time in preparing for the voyage." He wrote to the Directors that he had resolved to leave India within a month, wishing rather to avoid the receipt of orders regarding the new system of government than to await their

arrival, as they were not likely to concern him personally. "I consider myself," he added, "in this act as the
fortunate instrument of dissolving the frame of an inefficient government, pernicious to your interests, and
disgraceful to the national character." With this parting
benediction on the cranky vessel, ill made, ill manned,
hard to steer, sail, or keep afloat in foul weather, which
he had commanded with mutinous officers, short provisions, and inefficient machinery through the storms and
straits of eleven years, Warren Hastings laid down his
Governor-Generalship, " after a service of thirty-five years
from its commencement, and almost thirteen of them
passed in the charge and exercise of the first nominal
office of this government."

He left the shores of India in February, 1785. Many
valedictory addresses, and an universal expression of
regret at his departure, attested the great honour and
esteem in which he was indisputably held by all classes
of the community ; nor can there be any doubt that
throughout Northern India he had the highest reputation
as a statesman and an administrator. Forbes, who,
though a contemporary of Hastings, never served under
him, relates in his *Oriental Memoirs* how he was visited
on the west coast of India by a Brahmin pilgrim, who
said that he had been travelling all over the country and
found that the natives were far better off under Hastings'
government than under any other rule. And it is on
record that at the time when Hastings was most harassed
by personal broils and public anxieties, any man, English
or native, who had business with him might speak to
him from six in the morning up to eight at night ; a
sure way to popularity for officials in India. There is

N

also, among other testimonies, the evidence given on the trial by Lord Cornwallis, his successor in the Governor-Generalship, who said that Hastings was much esteemed and respected by the natives in the provinces under the Bengal government; and Sir John Shore, afterwards Lord Teignmouth, an Indian officer of the highest character, deposed to the same effect.

The subjoined extract from a contemporary native historian, whose work is not without some general merit, is taken out of Elliott's materials for the *History of India*. It gives the popular version then current in India of the circumstances and causes of the Governor-General's departure. It is also of some interest to the critical historian as illustrating the mistakes of fact and the total misconception of contemporary events into which even a fairly well-informed annalist may fall who relies, like all early chroniclers, mainly on hearsay and current report.

" Mr. Hastings, who some years previously had been appointed by the King of England as Governor of Bengal, Maksúdábàd, and Patna, revolted from his obedience, and paid no attention to the king's orders, declaring that he was a servant of the kings of India. The King of England sent another to Calcutta in his place ; and when he arrived in Calcutta and went to visit Mr. Hastings that gentleman killed him by the power of his sorceries. After this the King of England despatched another officer to fill the place of Mr. Hastings at Calcutta, but that gentleman declined to resign charge of the government. At last they determined on fighting a duel, with the understanding that the victor should assume the office of Governor. A day was fixed, and on that day they fought a duel. Mr. Hastings escaped, but wounded his antagonist in the arm with a pistol-ball, who was consequently obliged to return to England. The King of England then contrived a plot, and sent to Calcutta about four hundred

European soldiers in a vessel under the command of Mr. Macpherson, with a letter to Mr. Hastings to the effect that, as in these days he had many battles to fight, Mr. Macpherson had been despatched with these soldiers to reinforce him and to render service to him whenever exigency might require it. Secret instructions were given to Mr. Macpherson and the soldiers to seize Mr. Hastings and to forward him to His Majesty's presence. When the ship reached near Calcutta Mr. Macpherson sent the royal letter to Mr. Hastings, and saluted him with the fire of guns of the ship.   Mr. Hastings, having read the letter, embarked in a boat, and, in company of the other English officers who were with him in Calcutta, proceeded to welcome Mr. Macpherson.   On his approaching the vessel Mr. Macpherson paid a salute and with a double guard of the European soldiers went from the ship into Mr. Hastings' boat.   Immediately on boarding the boat, he ordered the soldiers to surround Mr. Hastings, and having thus made him a prisoner, showed him the orders for his own appointment as Governor, and the warrant which His Majesty had given for the apprehension of Mr. Hastings, who saw no remedy but to surrender himself a prisoner.   Mr. Macpherson sent him to England in a ship under the custody of the European guard which had come out for that purpose."

CHAPTER VIII

THE IMPEACHMENT AND TRIAL

DURING his voyage home Hastings sketched out a review of the state of Bengal, which on reaching England he gave to Mr. Dundas, who professed to have derived much instruction from it. This paper may be taken partly as an account of his stewardship, of the condition and prospects of his government in its various branches at the time when he quitted it, and partly as a retrospect and political testament. In this review he estimates the revenues of Bengal at five and a half millions sterling, and the public debt at three millions; and he shows that at the end of a war maintained during five years with the Mahrattas, the Mysore rulers, and latterly with the French, after having sent two large armies "to the extremities of Hindustan and the Deccan," after having supplied the heavy demands of the other Presidencies and maintained the commercial investments for England, the debt of Bengal stood at little more than half the annual income. Two years after the peace, he observed, the unfunded debt alone of Great Britain was thirty-six millions; but the Indian government had no such public credit as could provide their war expenditure from loans, and the financial distress of Bengal had been caused by the habit of regarding its revenues as an inexhaustible

fund upon which the rest of British India might draw
without limit.   It was this inability to borrow in times
of emergency that drove Hastings to raise money by
forced loans and war contributions in Benares and Oude ;
for the natives of India were in those days unaccustomed
to lend upon a public security, and indeed put less trust
in princes than in any other class of borrower.

Hastings takes in this review a rapid survey of the
state of the relations between Bengal and the native
powers ; showing remarkable breadth of view and
political prescience in his reflections upon the general
position of the British nation in India, in explaining the
scope and design of his own administrative plans, and in
defending himself from the charges of ambition and a
love of conquest.   Touching the origin and growth of
the Company's power in India he says : " The seed of
this wonderful production was sown by the hand of
calamity ; it was nourished by fortune, and cultivated
and shaped by necessity."   So firmly, nevertheless, had
this plant taken root in a few years, that the late war
had proved to all the leading powers of India " that their
combined strength and politics, assisted by our great
enemy the French, have not been able to destroy the
solid fabric of the English power in the East, nor even
to deprive it of any portion of its territories."   He
affirmed, and his judgment has been fully upheld by
events, that India needed " nothing but attention, protection, and forbearance "; an equal, vigorous, and fixed
administration, and free play for its vast natural resources
and advantages, to secure its rapid rise to a high and permanent level of national prosperity.   " But while," he
added, " I profess on these grounds the doctrine of peace,

I have never yet sacrificed to it by yielding a substantial right which I could assert, or submitting to a wrong which I could repel, with a moral assurance of success proportionate to the magnitude of either, and I should have deemed it criminal not to have hazarded both the public safety and my own in a crisis of uncommon and adequate emergency, or in an occasion of dangerous example."

"I have ever deemed it even more unsafe than dishonourable to sue for peace ; and more consistent with the love of peace to be the aggressor, in certain cases, than to see preparations of intended hostility, and to wait for their maturity, and for their open effect to repel it. The faith of treaties I have ever held inviolate. But I have had the satisfaction of seeing the policy, as well as the moral rectitude, of this practice justified by the exemplary sufferings of all who have deviated from it, in acts of perfidy to myself or to the government over which I have presided."

He goes on to press, as a point incontestable, the impossibility of British India being ruled by a body of men variable in their succession, discordant in their opinion, jealous of each other, and often united in common interest against their ostensible leader ; and he insists on the positive necessity of investing the Governor-General with the superior power that was in fact conferred upon his successor. To the hopes that he had entertained of exercising such powers, and of becoming the instrument of raising the British name and the worth of our Indian possessions to a degree of prosperity proportional to such a trust, he alludes as to a dream that had vanished, leaving him "with the poor and only consolation of the conscious knowledge of what I could have effected, had my destiny ordained that I should attain the situation to which I aspired."

These passages are suffused and instinct with the glow
and spirit of the writer's character and temperament;
with his self-reliance, firmness of purpose, hardihood, and
ambition; showing a man capable of standing by friends
and against enemies, and indicating the dangerous and
slightly vindictive element in him that might come out
under close pressure.[1] They illustrate also his faculty
of looking through and beyond the passing clouds of
adverse circumstance and accidental failure by which
men are so easily blinded and dispirited, and of fixing
his eyes steadily on the main chances and essential conditions of success. He saw not only the sea of troubles
which encompassed the English in India, but the calm
and open waters that were to be reached by resolute and
skilful navigation. So long as he could keep the vessel's
head straight on the point to which he had set her,
neither waves nor wind, nor a mutiny on board, could
wrench the helm from his straining hands. His own
business had latterly been rather to save the ship than to
sail it; and he did save it at all personal hazards, risking
his reputation as freely as men risk their lives in a storm.
The rest of the great enterprise he was obliged to leave
to others; but he foresaw plainly the potency of expansion contained in the superiority already acquired by the
English in India, and the ease with which his successors
might realise his vision of a spacious, flourishing, and
pacific dominion.

Wraxall records in his *Memoirs* the appearance in
London of Mrs. Hastings, her gracious reception at

---

[1] " For though I am not splenetive or rash,
     Yet there is in me something dangerous
     Which let thy wisdom fear."—*Hamlet.*

Court, the society gossip about her antecedents, and the
malevolent criticism excited by her diamonds,[1] and by
her audacity in wearing her hair unpowdered when the
fashionable lady's head-dress was twelve or eighteen inches
high.   A year later he reports the arrival "from the
banks of the Ganges" of Governor-General Hastings.

"When he landed in his native country, he had attained
his fifty-second year. . . . In his person he was thin, but
not tall ; of a spare habit, very bald, with a countenance
placid and thoughtful, but when animated full of intelligence.
Never perhaps did any man who passed the Cape of Good
Hope display a mind more elevated above mercenary considerations.   Placed in a situation where he might have amassed
immense wealth without exciting censure, he revisited England
with only a modest competence. . . . In private life he was
playful and gay to a degree hardly conceivable, never carrying
his political vexations into the bosom of his family.   Of a
temper so buoyant and elastic, that the instant he quitted the
Council board, where he had been assailed by every species of
opposition, often heightened by personal acrimony, he mixed
in society like a youth upon whom care had never intruded."

Wraxall goes on to tell two anecdotes, too long for
insertion here, in evidence of the magnanimity and
generosity with which Hastings "looked down upon
pecuniary concerns."   The sketch is so far valuable that
it was drawn by a contemporary who knew Hastings,
and who was by no means inclined to defend all his
political acts.   And the favourable impression produced
by Hastings on his return home is corroborated by the
entries regarding him in the reminiscences of Nicholls,

---

[1] "Oh Pitt, with awe behold that precious throat
  Whose necklace teems with many a future vote !
  Pregnant with Burgage gems each hand she wears,
  And lo ! depending questions gleam upon her ears ! "
                                      Probationary Ode.

who like Wraxall was at that time in Parliament and in society, and who goes so far as to write, " I think that he was a man of the most powerful mind I ever conversed with."

Hastings landed in June, 1785, was much vexed at not finding his wife in London, rushed off toward Cheltenham after two days' stay, and on Maidenhead Bridge met her coming to meet him.   His first reception in England pleased and elated him greatly.   He wrote that he found himself everywhere and universally treated with evidences that he possessed the good opinion of his country ; the Directors formally thanked him for his services ; the Board of Control was more than polite ; the King and Queen received him most kindly ; and " Lord Thurlow has been more substantially my friend than King, Ministers, or Directors."   He remarked, however, that these very distinctions also made him an object of public calumny ; and so soon as in July he received a letter from the Court of Directors requiring him to furnish particulars of certain sums of money presented to him in 1782.   Nevertheless he seems to have fancied himself above danger, and fairly safe under the protection of those who had paid him so many compliments.   The English nation were not much accustomed at that period to see their governors or their generals return triumphantly ; they had witnessed the loss of colonies, the surrender of armies, and the failure of expeditions ; but here at least was a man who had preserved a great territory entrusted to him, and who had made it over in tranquillity and security to his successor.   Hastings, " whose whole life had been passed in Asia, and who very imperfectly knew the ground at St. James's or

Westminster, ignorantly supposed that his public merits
would at least balance any acts of severity, or any strong
measures to which he might have had recourse for the
purpose, not of enriching himself, but of replenishing the
exhausted treasury of Bengal. . . . "[1] "That a man
who had performed resplendent services should, instead
of finding himself decorated with honours on revisiting
his native country, meet an impeachment, that he should
be compared by Burke to Verres, and by Courtenay to
Cortez, may at first view create surprise"; but closer
inspection [Wraxall said] would show the causes. He
had numerous and powerful enemies, headed by Burke
and Fox, who not only stood pledged to press forward
the question of maladministration in India, but saw that
the movement would give their party a tactical advantage
in the contest with Pitt and Dundas. The Ministers
would be placed in a dilemma; for while they could hardly
oppose a demand for inquiry without laying themselves
under suspicion of conniving at Indian delinquencies,
by joining in the attack on Hastings they would risk
their favour with the king and might be deserted by
some of their supporters. There was indeed no lack of
significant and ominous warnings that might have dis-
quieted Hastings. Francis, "an implacable and able
adversary," supplied local information ; and the league
against him was joined by all the friends of Clavering,
Monson, and Macartney. In February, only a few
months before his return, Burke had taunted Scott
with being Hastings' agent; and Scott retaliated by
accusing Burke of being himself virtually a minister
of the Rajah of Tanjore ; alluding to the position

[1] Wraxall, *Memoirs*, i. 336.

of William Burke at the Tanjore Court. This roused
Burke to declare, truly and impressively, that his
long exertions for the oppressed and unfortunate had
never received any pecuniary compensation. And a fortnight later he delivered his speech on the Nawab of
Arcot's debts, in which he thundered against the criminal
prodigality and venal subservience to corrupt peculators
that he detected in the Ministerial proposals for the
settlement of these debts, taunted Pitt with showering
gold, like Nero on his prætorians, on his Indian adherents,
and solemnly bound himself over to spare no pains in
prosecuting a full and severe inquiry into Indian affairs.
Pitt treated with disdainful silence the attack on his
own integrity, but he made no attempt to defend the
Indian government; and during the rest of that year
Burke was concerting with Fox and Francis the ways
and means of bringing the whole question before Parliament. The House of Commons, he wrote to Francis,
had conceived a favourable opinion of Hastings, and very
favourable wishes for him; "they will not judge of his
intentions by his acts, but will qualify his acts by his
presumed intentions"; the condemnation of Hastings he
believed then to be impracticable, and he only hoped to
obtain a respectable minority for his own acquittance and
justification. By December, 1785, he had sent to Francis
his draft of "the first scene of the first act," the Rohilla
war; Lord Macartney came home in January, 1786, full of
hostility to the late Governor-General, and disappointed
in his expectation of succeeding him; while Hastings,
unconscious of the gathering clouds, was travelling about
England, negotiating for the purchase of Daylesford,
and corresponding with Dundas and Thurlow about the

revision of Pitt's India Act. He had heard that Pitt was
withholding his honours on the plea that Burke was still
threatening some charges. "Whether this man," Hastings wrote, "really means what he has threatened I know
not, having heard nothing about him for many months;
nor have I ever made him the subject of my inquiries."

When George the Third opened Parliament in January,
1786, his Ministry was led by the most powerful and
triumphant chief that ever headed a strong majority in
the Commons.   But Pitt was also confronted by opponents of the highest intellectual genius and of consummate
excellence in debate, smarting under an ignominious
defeat upon an Indian question, and fighting desperately
to retrieve it.   In European politics there was a perceptible lull after the termination of a wide-spreading war;
and at home the vicissitudes of party strife had concentrated public attention upon the affairs of India, and
upon the conduct of its English administrators.   It was
at this conjuncture that the devouring zeal of Major
Scott impelled him to rise, toward the close of the first
day of Parliament's meeting, for the purpose of remind-
ing Burke of his engagement at the last session to bring
forward charges against Hastings, and of asking him to
fix a time for proceeding, if he meant to proceed at all,
as the late Governor-General felt the utmost anxiety
for despatch.   Fox rose first in reply to assure Scott
that the business should not be neglected; and Burke
coolly answered that a general did not consult his
enemies as to the place or occasion for a battle.   This
sounded ominous enough to those who knew something
of the fires underlying the deceptive crust on which
Hastings was standing; and every one can now see that

the challenge was a tremendous blunder on the part of his friends.   In February Burke rose, and desired that the resolutions moved by Dundas in 1782 for the censure and recall of Hastings might be read to the House; after which he moved for certain papers necessary to the framing of the impeachment, saying that he was called upon and driven to the business which he was now engaged to prosecute.   Wraxall believed, with many others, that if Scott had never written or spoken in the House for Hastings, the latter would never have been impeached; but he adds that recent Parliamentary history ought to have forewarned him that he was on dangerous ground.   Hastings relied for security, if not for recompense, on three foundations, all of which proved totally without solidity.   The first was his public services; the second, royal favour; the last, Ministerial support.   But the verdict on his services depended on whether they were judged by political expediency, or by such a rigorous moral standard as is rarely applied to the acts of men who have to face imminent public danger.   As to royal favour, "George the Third could extend no protection to a man impeached by the Commons of Great Britain"; while Pitt, Dundas, and Jenkinson, the Cabinet leaders in Parliament, had no mind to stake their position on the defence of Indian administration, or to baulk the Opposition in starting at full cry after other game than His Majesty's Ministers. Wraxall adds truly that what had saved Clive from a similar prosecution was that his services were not civil but military, and that he took care not to provoke Parliamentary scrutiny.

During the month of March Burke moved several

times for papers connected with his charges against
Hastings, whose conduct in regard to the Mahratta war
Pitt and Dundas defended, declaring that the treaty
which ended it saved the British empire in Asia.   In
the meantime Scott skirmished with Fox and Sheridan,
taunting the former with having denounced Lord North,
his present colleague, quite as vehemently as he now
accused Hastings, and exasperating both of them by his
allegations that they had offered in 1784 to accommodate
matters with Hastings as a bargain for the support of
Fox's India Bill by the friends of the Governor-General.
Then the Act to confer upon the Governor-General in
India power to overrule his Council, which Dundas
passed on appointing Lord Cornwallis, brought out
Burke with a demonstration in force against a measure
which he styled the establishment of a Turkish tyranny
throughout our Eastern dominions, of a new Star
Chamber (the Board of Control) for the subversion of
Magna Charta; while on the other side the word Impeachment had produced several rancorous allusions to
Burke's previous intentions of impeaching Lord North,
"the noble lord in the blue ribbon" who now sat beside
him.   So by the time that Hastings appeared at the
bar of the House of Commons to be heard in his own
defence, the temper of the Opposition had grown hot and
fierce, and their leaders had staked their reputation on
a rigorous prosecution.   It is now generally agreed that
the first step made by Hastings, in applying to be heard
in his own defence, was a mistake.   Lord Clive had
been defended in similar circumstances by Wedderburn,
a consummate advocate; and Rigby, an adroit and
unscrupulous Parliamentary tactician, had undertaken

the congenial task of pleading for Sir Thomas Rumbold,
who was himself a member of the House of Commons.
But Hastings committed the serious error of appearing
in person to read for hours a long exculpatory paper
of general observations upon the method and manner of
the prosecution, and of separate replies to the particular
charges.   In the tone of a man injured and ill requited
for his services he spoke of his surprise at finding himself
arraigned there as a criminal, when he had left India
unanimously regretted by princes and people, and had
received the thanks of the Directors and the approval
of the Court of Proprietors, "in whose applause alone
I receive a consolation under all my discouragements.
. . . With such testimonies in my favour, and with the
internal applause of my own mind superseding all evidence, what was my surprise to find, on my arrival in
England, that my character still continued to be assailed
by the bitterest calumnies and invectives.   Though I
might have thought myself entitled by my services to a
different reception, and though I might erroneously
imagine that no power on earth had a right to impeach
me for the exercise of a trust which those for whom
I had held it had repeatedly declared that I had dis-
charged to their benefit and entire satisfaction, yet I
was glad to see some substantial ground for hope of a
speedy trial." He complained of the delay in producing
the charges; and went on into prolix and complicated
explanations of the real nature and circumstances of the
transactions with the Rajah and Begums of Benares,
and of other details connected with the accusations
against him.

The effect, says Wraxall, upon a popular assembly

accustomed to splendid displays of eloquence, was lame
and tedious after the first hour; and the tone of his
exordium rather put the Commons on their mettle to
show what they thought of Directors and Proprietors,
and of men whom the East India Company delighted
to honour. The reading of this defence took up two
days, which the House thought too long and Hastings
much too short; and it elicited on its termination only
a few words from Burke, who in June opened fire
in earnest with the Rohilla war charge; preluding with
the observation that the drift of the defence was to
demur to the jurisdiction of Parliament, and to imply
that a Governor-General was answerable only to his
employers, the East India Company. He was supported
by an effective and forcible speech from Fox, and followed by Hardinge, Solicitor-General to the Queen,
whose severe criticism on the style of the defence
appears to have impressed Pitt. "I see in it," he said,
"a perfect character drawn by the culprit himself, and
that character is his own. Conscious triumph in the
ability and success of all his measures pervades every
sentence." There was undoubtedly something provok-
ing in the unswerving faith with which Hastings invariably maintained that he had always done what he
ought to have done, and appealed to a conscience that
never failed to acquit him fully of blame or blunder.
But Hastings had been three times named by Parliament Governor-General of Bengal after the Rohilla
war; so this charge was opposed by the Government, and rejected by a large Ministerial majority,
whereupon the friends of the accused were loudly jubi-
lant, but prematurely; for Pitt had said nothing, and so

many members had absented themselves that the vote
had been taken in a thin House.   It was soon evident
that everything would depend upon the line taken by
Pitt and Dundas in respect to the next charge against
Hastings, which went upon his treatment of the Rajah of
Benares.   In the debate upon that article Pitt spoke at
length.   He censured the language of the prosecution as
violent and unfair : he declared that the conduct of
Francis, who had acquiesced in proceedings which he
now imputed as a crime to Hastings, was malignant and
tortuous ; and he praised the high qualities shown by
Hastings in great emergencies.   Nevertheless, he said,
he should agree to the motion, because although he flatly
rejected the doctrine of Cheyt Singh's sovereign independence, and allowed that he might be called upon for
a subsidy, yet the fine, though justifiable in principle,
was in amount exorbitant, unjust, and tyrannical.
Wraxall, who was present, writes that the astonishment
produced by so unexpected a declaration would be
difficult to describe ; and Lord Mahon tells us that when
Pitt rose, and indeed for a long time afterward, the
House had been firmly persuaded of his intention to
side with Hastings.   A Treasury circular had been sent
to all the supporters of the Government, asking them to
attend and vote against Fox's motion ; and the turn, says
Lord Campbell, was so sudden that the Attorney-General
divided against the Prime Minister, while several prominent men in office professed their inability to follow
his conversion.   But the Ministerialists as a body voted
with their chief, and Hastings was condemned by one
hundred and nineteen against seventy-nine.

    Macaulay in his essay treats the ostensible reason

put forward by Pitt for his vote on this occasion, which
determined the impeachment, as totally inadequate and
unworthy of the Prime Minister's great ability. That
contemporary opinion took the same view is proved by
the variety of rumours and conjectures of occult causes
and veiled motives to which his sudden change of attitude
gave currency. There is the story, told thirty years
later by Hastings himself as a well-attested anecdote,
of Dundas having visited Pitt early that morning, and
having persuaded him after three hours' discussion to
abandon Hastings : there is the suggestion that Dundas
was jealous of Hastings as a probable rival at the Board
of Control ; and there is Lord Campbell's story of Pitt
having received, a few hours before the debate began,
intelligence of Thurlow's assertion that he would put
the Great Seal to a patent for Hastings' peerage under
the king's authority, without consulting the minister.
All these tales may have some truth in them, and the
last of them, if authentic, would go far to account for
Pitt's action in the matter ; for nothing could have been
more calculated to irritate him than Thurlow's ostentatious
patronage of Hastings, or a threat of dealing with the
king over his head. Nor would Pitt have been likely
to be better pleased at the special favour shown by their
Majesties to Mr. and Mrs. Hastings, which gave rise to
scandalous insinuations against all concerned, to squibs
and lampoons, and to very disagreeable doubts and sur-
mises regarding Pitt's own independence of Court influences, a point upon which he was particularly sensitive.
On the day after the debate on the Benares charge, a big
diamond sent by the Nizam of Hyderabad to the king
was formally presented at a levée which was attended

by Hastings ; an unlucky incident that attracted much
public remark, and naturally formed a capital subject
for broad political caricature. It is also worth notice
that six months later, when Burke was pressing for the
nomination of Francis upon the impeachment committee,
he conveyed, in a letter to Dundas, a formal warning to
Pitt that his personal reputation was committed to the
business of the impeachment, and that there would be
danger to his ministry in allowing Hastings and his
friends to triumph and to form a political party in the
country. Very possibly this may not have been then
said or thought for the first time ; and on the whole it
is a reasonable conclusion that Pitt and Dundas, of whom
the former always looked coldly on Hastings and the
latter had censured and condemned him, did resolve,
after private consultation, not to stand between Hastings
and his powerful accusers at the risk of some loss of
political character and some strain upon their ascendency in the House and the country.

The clouds were now gathering thick and heavy
round Hastings.   In the next session of Parliament
(February, 1787) Sheridan delivered that famous speech
upon the case of the Begums of Oude, in which, according
to the universal opinion of his contemporaries, he rose
to the highest water-mark of English eloquence ; which
was heard with intense attention during five hours, left
the audience breathless with admiration, and produced a
decisive effect on the whole House.   His pathetic invoca-
tions, allusions, and exclamations ; his impassioned
invectives and appeals ; his dramatic narratives and
copious metaphors, the profusion of colouring and
imagery — all these things seem to have enchanted,

captivated, and finally convinced the most renowned
assembly of orators and statesmen in the world. Yet
the few sentences preserved by Wraxall, whose admiration of the speech is unqualified, may appear to modern
taste somewhat disappointing. Hastings is called a
mixture of the trickster and the tyrant, at once Scapin
and Dionysius : his policy is crooked as the curves of a
writhing snake; he is likened to a highwayman, to a
felon kite, to a man holding in one hand a bloody sceptre
while with the other he picks pockets ; and almost every
crime which can stain or debase human nature is attributed to him. However this may be, Fox declared that
all he had ever read or heard of in oratory, either in the
House or elsewhere, sank to nothing in comparison with
Sheridan's speech. Scott vainly attempted to counteract
its impression by pointing out perversions of fact, by
pleas of urgent political necessity, and by enumerating
the meritorious public acts of the man accused. Pitt
admitted the resumption of the *jágírs* to be justifiable,
but he censured the seizure of the Begums' treasure ;
the Ministers voted against Hastings, and he was condemned by a still larger majority than before. Political
necessity will serve as a palliation for irregularities in
proportion as the sense of peril is strong in the national
mind; but as this feeling fades the plea rapidly loses
force, and when the danger is distant or forgotten public
morality recovers its ordinary elevation. The only
speech in Hastings' favour that had for a moment checked
the Parliamentary attacks on him was made by a distinguished admiral, Lord Hood, who told the House that
he himself should have ended his days in prison if the
Government had not stood between him and prosecutions

for illegal acts done to preserve his fleet during the late
war, and who conjured the House to hesitate before
punishing too severely a man who had elected rather
to incur personal risks than the chances of failure in
preserving a distant province in the midst of a general
war. But the time had passed for holding this ground
effectively against furious charges of cruelty or corruption ; the doctrine of a set-off, of balancing good deeds
against errors, was evidently inapplicable to such accusations ; and, moreover, it had been distinctly repudiated
as much by Hastings himself as by the prosecutors, for
Hastings insisted that his conduct had been not only
pardonable but meritorious. Pitt in replying to Admiral
Hood laid stress on this point, observing that Hastings
had disclaimed all benefit arising from the consideration
of his services, "being persuaded that the very facts on
which are founded the charges will, upon investigation,
be found entitled to the approbation of this House." It
was this curious incapacity of Hastings to place himself
in the mental attitude of those who discerned flaws in
his conduct, that exposed him to the attacks of his
accusers. He was like a man who should throw away a
shield and disdain the arts of fence through belief in his
own invulnerability. When, therefore, the issue whether
he deserved praise or blame for certain specific acts was
placed before the House of Commons, it was easily
determined, with the assent of the Ministers, in favour
of an impeachment. Pitt nominated Burke to be the
first member of the Committee of Impeachment ; but
when Burke proceeded to nominate Philip Francis, Pitt
joined the majority in rejecting him as a notorious and
implacable enemy of the accused ; a decision against

which Burke protested strenuously, feeling, he said, the cause to be in some degree damned by it. The Ministry supported the second reading of the articles of impeachment, which was carried after an acrimonious discussion ; and in May, 1787, Burke, attended by a great number of the members present, formally impeached Warren Hastings at the bar of the House of Lords. He was taken into custody by the sergeant-at-arms, and held to bail for £20,000, with sureties for £10,000[1] each ; but the trial in Westminster Hall did not begin until February 13th in the following year.

The House of Lords is a court of justice in which peers and commoners may be tried for offences upon an impeachment (*impetitio*) by the House of Commons, which is the grand jury of the whole nation. The power of impeachment was the weapon by which the Parliament leaders fought their battle from 1640 to 1642 ; but in the eighteenth century its importance declined, and it became a subject rather of constitutional and antiquarian curiosity than of practical use.[2] It is manifest that such a tribunal was eminently adapted to invest its proceedings with the ceremonial splendour and dignified solemnity that exalt and harmonise with fine oratorical displays, and to fix the attention of a nation that has always been enormously interested in State trials, which have been the pictures that illustrate the national history. The spectacle at the opening of the impeachment has been described by Macaulay in a famous passage ; and Debrett's history of the trial published in 1796 contains a plan of the High Court of Parliament erected

---

[1] Gleig says £2000 and £1000.

[2] Stephen, *History of Criminal Law*, i. 146.

in Westminster Hall, showing the arrangement of the
seats, the places and names of the principal persons who
were there, and even the dresses of the ladies. Warren
Hastings was summoned and appeared at the bar, looking
"very infirm and much indisposed ; he was dressed in a
plain poppy-coloured suit of clothes"; he dropped on
his knees, and was told by the Lord Chancellor that he
might rise. After proclamation had been made requiring
all persons concerned to make good their charges, the
Lord Chancellor (Thurlow), who had throughout been
prepossessed very favourably toward Hastings, made him a
short address that seems intended to convey an assurance
that the high authority and adverse temper of the Commons should not prejudice his fair trial ; "for the matter
in the charges is most momentous, and the dates are
remote since the occurrences alleged against you in those
charges are said to have been committed."

Twenty articles of charge, with Hastings' answer and
the Commons' replication, were then read ; and upon the
third day Mr. Burke, standing forth, as he said, at the
command of the Commons of England to accuse Warren
Hastings, began a speech which occupied in delivery the
next four days, concluding with the impassioned peroration of which Macaulay has given the final comminatory
sentences. It was an introductory address reviewing
the history of India, the system of government under
the Company, and in particular the administration of
Hastings ; and he thence passed to a preliminary account
of the charges that were to be proved against the accused,
rising gradually from a grave and temperate narrative to
the highest pitch of tragic declamation. He described
with all the force and fire of his magnificent phraseology

the cruel tortures which certain native revenue officers
appointed by the Governor-General were reported to have
inflicted upon peasants in Bengal ; and he denounced
Hastings with having knowingly appointed as his sub-
servient tools the diabolical authors of these atrocities ;
"with having thereby wasted the country, destroyed the
landed interest, cruelly harassed the peasants, burned
their houses, seized their crops, tortured and degraded
their persons, and destroyed the honour of the whole
female race of that country." He also charged him with
fraud, bribery, and robbery ; adjuring all bishops, judges,
and nobles there present to avenge the cause of oppressed
princes, of undone women of the first rank, of desolated
provinces and wasted kingdoms, by punishing impiety,
injustice, dishonour, and the violation of all power and
institutions.

Wraxall, who was present, writes in his *Memoirs* that
the oration is unequalled, he believes, either in antiquity
or in modern days. "It will be difficult to convey an
idea of the agitation, distress, and horror excited among
the female part of his audience by his statement of the
atrocities and, in many instances, the deeds of blood per-
petrated, as Burke asserted, by Hastings' connivance or by
his express command." The whole audience were powerfully stirred, and there was great emotion among the
ladies ; yet it is doubtful whether such a rhetorical exhi-
bition could have profoundly impressed the cooler hearts
and stronger nerves of those present who understood
what is meant by evidence when a man's life and honour
are in jeopardy ; and the performance illustrates forcibly
the changes of taste and style, so easy to mark and so
hard to explain, that are constantly going on among us.

In our own days a governor or a general would rightly
be held responsible for the misdeeds of his subordinates,
when he might have foreseen, prevented, or discovered
them ; nor can a political party leader easily escape discredit and dishonour if his followers openly rejoice in
sedition, rebellion, and assassination.   But if at a great
judicial investigation held at the present time the imputation of such a responsibility were made a pretext
for denouncing a prominent personage in the terms used
by Burke and Sheridan, the manœuvre would only excite
scorn and disgust, and would be fatal to the cause of
those who employed it.   Some such effect, indeed, was
probably produced by the violence of the attack upon
Hastings.   The Lord Chancellor commented upon the
circumstances of accumulated horror that had been described, and upon the acts of atrocity that had been imputed to the accused, and intimated that the management
would be held to the proof of all that had been asserted.
And Mr. Law, the leading counsel for the defence,
ventured upon some protest against the harshness of the
language used by the prosecution ; but although he,
Dallas, and Plumer were all men of high professional
reputation, it was unfortunate for Hastings that Erskine,
whose unrivalled eloquence as an advocate best qualified
him to confront the brilliant staff of orators who led the
attack, had been deterred from accepting the brief by
his reluctance to appear in a political case against the
chiefs of his own party.

Before the speeches began, the answer of Hastings to
the charges had been read ; it was the same as that which
he had himself recited in the House of Commons.   Burke,
in opening the impeachment, alludes contemptuously to

"that indecent and unbecoming paper which lies on our table"; yet although it is not a model of judicious pleading, the answer contains matter for the attention and even the sympathy of a dispassionate reader.

"In truth," he said, "the articles are not charges, but histories and comments. They are yet more; they are made up of mutilated quotations, of facts which have no mutual relation but are forced by false arrangement into connection, of principles of pernicious policy and false morality; assertions of guilt without proof or the attempt to prove them; interpretations of secret motives and designs which passed within my own breast, and which none but myself would know. . . .

"With respect to the general subject of the charge I must beg leave to observe that it has been composed from a laboured scrutiny of my whole official life, during a most important and weighty administration of thirteen years, comprehending perhaps a greater variety of interesting events than have fallen to the lot of any man now living; events not brought to the public view by their notoriety alone, but all the subject of minute record. . . . All my actions have undergone, and even during their actual progress they underwent, such a severity of investigation as could suit only a mind possessing in itself an absolute exemption from error. In the present occasion I am put to a harder test; for not my actions alone, but my words, and even my imputed thoughts, as at the final day of judgment, are converted into accusation against me. And from whom is this state of perfection exacted? From a man who was separated, while yet but a schoolboy, from his native country, and from every advantage of that instruction which might have better qualified him for the high offices and arduous situations which it became his lot to fill."

It seems hardly possible that this appeal to his fellow-countrymen, although the style may have been a little out of fashion, should not have touched the sentiment of fair play and of consideration due to men who have at

least shown high courage and patriotic spirit in the
public service, and who, after facing tremendous odds
for their country, are brought by their country to fight
at the same odds for themselves. Such a situation is
well known in the annals of men of action, and popular
governments are wayward masters; but on the whole
the British nation has not much taste for reviling men
who have carried its flag high in foreign lands. That
the Committee of Impeachment should not have been
troubled with these feelings is in no way a matter of
surprise or of blame upon them. They were pledged to
push on a great public prosecution : their own reputation and their political interests were staked upon its
success; and the chief managers had sincerely convinced
themselves of its justice and necessity. If Hastings had
for thirteen years been contending against difficulties
in India, in England Burke had for fourteen years been
indefatigably labouring to check the disorders of Indian
administration, and to bring Indian affairs under effective
Parliamentary control. Now at last, as he believed, he
had brought the chief offender to bay, and was closing in
upon him, sore and exasperated with the fatigues and
disappointments of a long chase. Nevertheless the
unsparing vigour of the prosecutors, the language in
which they endeavoured to inflame the minds of such a
judicial body as the House of Lords and of the audience,
and to hound on the nation against the prisoner, and
their disregard of those precautions required for a proper
scrutiny of unfamiliar circumstances and complex Oriental
transactions, were unworthy of such large-minded statesmen as Burke and Fox, and must be accounted for by
the pressure of a political atmosphere which was heated

and tempestuous to a degree unknown even in the rather stormy Parliamentary weather of our own times.

The first charge was opened by Fox in a speech that was much more moderate in tone, and closer in its reasoning, than Burke's introductory address. And in June Sheridan took up the second charge regarding the treatment of the Begums of Oude, upon which he dilated for several successive days in a speech that was manifestly much better adapted to the intellectual form and fashion of those days than of the present time. It would be most presumptuous to suppose that Sheridan did not know how best to persuade and please the House of Lords; but if the summary of this oration has been fairly given in Debrett's history of the trial, the modern reader will probably be startled at the quantity of declamation, invocation, metaphor, humorous illustration, and caricature that is employed to throw a glaring light upon a sufficiently ill-favoured business, and to overdrive the true arguments for condemning the Governor-General's part in it. No one in these days uses irony and bitter sarcasm against a prisoner on his trial, nor is it thought fair or judicious to introduce grotesque figures of speech or degrading comparisons. Nevertheless Gibbon wrote to Lord Sheffield that Sheridan had in this speech surpassed himself; but Sheridan had coupled Gibbon with Tacitus, and had paid him the well-known compliment of an allusion to his luminous (or vo-luminous) pages. Horace Walpole said that the orator had not quite satisfied the passionate expectations of the people who had given fifty guineas for a ticket to hear him, although he wished that the Empress Catherine of Russia and Joseph of Austria, who were just then lacerating Turkey

by a bloody and unjust war, could be brought to Westminster Hall and worried by Sheridan.   At the close of
his address he sank, as is well known, into the arms of
Burke; and the Court, having sat thirty-five days in
1788, rose and adjourned to the next session of Parliament. In the meantime Fox had brought to the notice
of the Commons a pamphlet published by one Stockdale,[1]
containing, as he averred, highly disreputable and
indecent observations upon the motives which had
induced the House to impeach Hastings; and upon an
address by the House a criminal information was filed
against the publisher.   But Stockdale was defended by
Erskine, who showed on this occasion what he might
have done had he been Hastings' advocate; for he took
the opportunity of vindicating Hastings in a speech of
remarkable vigour and forensic dexterity, not denying
that Hastings had acted despotically, but arguing that
only the force wielded and the fear inspired by arbitrary
rule could maintain a distant, alien, and usurped dominion.

"If England," he said, "from a lust of ambition and
dominion, will insist on maintaining despotic rule over distant
and hostile nations beyond all comparison more numerous
and extended than herself, and gives commissions to her
viceroys to govern them, with no other instructions than to
preserve them and to secure permanently their revenues—
with what colour or consistency of reason can she place herself in the moral chair, and affect to be shocked at the
execution of her own orders?"

To this it may of course be answered that, in the present time at any rate, England *does* give other instructions,
very plainly and firmly, to her viceroys; but the argu-

---

[1] A bookseller in Piccadilly.   It was written by Logan, a Scotch
minister of some repute.

ment had a sufficiency of truth and a good popular ring
of fair play about it. And when Erskine drew a picture
of the trial in Westminster Hall, where "a terrible,
unceasing, exhaustless artillery of warm zeal, match-
less vigour of understanding, consuming and devouring
eloquence, was daily pouring forth upon one private
unprotected man," he succeeded in convincing the
jury that while the Commons were thus engaged they
were scarcely in a position to resent and punish a few
reflections on themselves. Stockdale was acquitted, and
Burke wrote to Francis that this verdict, coupled with
another in a libel case concerning Impey, had the air of
a "determination of the public voice against us." He
confessed, writing in 1789, that he totally despaired,
and thought of nothing but an honourable retreat from
the business, which was already becoming to some extent
a burden on all who had taken part in it. Other episodes
varied and prolonged the proceedings. Hastings had complained by petition to the Commons that Burke, speaking
on the trial, had said that he (Hastings) had murdered
Nuncomar by the hands of Sir Elijah Impey ; and during
the sharp debate on the question of receiving the petition, Fox observed that the managers might have shared
Nuncomar's fate if Impey had been their Chief-Justice.
Finally the Commons resolved, by a majority, that Burke's
words ought not to have been used ; whereupon Burke
told the Lords in Westminster Hall that the poverty of
the English language had led him to express his private
feelings by a word insufficient to convey an impression
of complicated atrocity, and that he had only used the
word "murder" in a moral and popular sense. The proceedings, delayed by the king's illness, were not reopened

until April, 1789, when Burke alluded to some public
curiosity as to the calculable duration of the trial, and
observed, with regard to some complaint by Hastings of
the cost, that a prisoner who had amassed an immense
fortune by bribes and peculation would hardly feel the
loss of £30,000. This year the trial went on for only
seventeen days.

When the Lord Chancellor was about to adjourn,
Hastings humbly asked their Lordships to consider that
"not one tenth part of one single article of the twenty
which compose the charge had been brought to a conclusion on the part of the prosecution only"; that he
had every prospect of passing the remainder of his life
under impeachment and of suffering far more severely
than if he had pleaded guilty at first. The Lord
Chancellor gave a civil answer; and in the House of
Lords the Earl of Camden spoke sympathetically of
the position not only of the prisoner but of their Lordships generally, who were bound to sit out the trial,
although many of them would be dead before it ended.
Nevertheless in the following year (1790) the Lords sat
no longer than a fortnight, which was taken up with
Fox's speech on the charges of internal maladministration and corruption, and with incessant disputes on
points of the admissibility of evidence, which had
usually to be referred to the judges. Burke moved the
House of Commons for steps to expedite matters;
while Scott wrote in Woodfall's Diary a letter attacking
the managers for cumbrous and dilatory procedure,
thereby bringing down upon himself a formal reprimand
from the Commons, who pronounced his writing to be
scandalous and libellous. The meeting of a new Parlia-

ment in November, 1790, raised the question, which was discussed at length in both Houses, whether an impeachment did not end and abate with a dissolution. Burke asked whether lawyers who confined their ideas to the narrow limits of a Nisi Prius trial were better able to ascertain what ought to be the end of an impeachment than a rabbit, who breeds three times a year, was capable of judging of the time of gestation of an elephant. It was decided that the impeachment was unaffected and survived; so after nearly a year's interval the trial was again set in motion in May, 1791, when speeches were delivered and evidence given on the charges of prodigality, corruption, and favouritism in the award of contracts. Hastings again represented to the Court that he was now sixty years of age, had been four years their prisoner, loaded and tortured by the most virulent accusations; and that at the rate of progress hitherto made he had no human expectation of living to make his defence, or to hear their Lordships' judgment. Burke and Fox replied by justifying strong language in the statement of strong facts, and said, not untruly, that the delay was none of their making. On the next day only eighteen lords were present; and at the end of May the prosecution was closed. Hastings then read a long statement of his defence, after which the Court adjourned, having sat only five days in the year 1791; although Lord King moved in the House of Lords that Parliament should not be prorogued until the trial had terminated, which would have very effectively shortened proceedings if the motion had not been indignantly negatived.

It was of course a task of extraordinary difficulty for

Hastings to reply comprehensively and yet concisely upon a case that had taken four years to be stated against him, and that had not been strictly limited to the articles charged, but had been extended and embellished by great orators who set the picture in a kind of framework of inhumanity and perfidy, and surrounded the real issues with dramatic narratives no less damaging than hard to disprove. Nevertheless the reply would be well worth reading if the reputation of Hastings still depended on the opinion that might be formed upon a study of these proceedings; and at any rate it illustrates his situation at this stage of the trial. For example, he says :

"Of thirty-four gentlemen who compose the list of witnesses whom I had originally selected for examination (in my defence) some are dead, some returned to their service in India, others, after an annual but fruitless and disheartening attendance, dispersed in unknown parts of these kingdoms, or in the remote regions of Europe. Those whose attendance I could engage are comparatively few in number, chiefly connected with me by habits of familiar intercourse, and their testimony for that very reason liable to be depreciated by the license which the managers have assumed with the characters of those, even of their own witnesses, whose evidence has not answered their expectations of it."

For this and other reasons he complains of "the unparalleled injury which I have suffered by the extension of a criminal trial beyond the chances of a life's duration"; and he declares to their Lordships that he is ready to waive his defence, if they will but graciously proceed to immediate judgment. As to the horrible cruelties of the native revenue officials which were charged upon him, he affirms that the worst of them were never committed at all, and that the accusation, so far as he was concerned, is an atrocious calumny which the managers could never be induced to bring forward in the form of an article of charge, although they were closely and repeatedly urged to do so. He persists somewhat too confidently, as usual, not only in denying that he had done wrong but also in affirming that he had done right, in regard to both Cheyt Singh and the Oude Begums. He declares that the funds obtained at Benares and Lucknow saved our Indian possessions by supplying our armies at their utmost need ; but he takes his stand on the ground that though his acts were justified by extreme necessity, they require no such justification. He concludes his address by drawing once more the contrast between his services and the treatment with which they had been requited.

"To the Commons of England, in whose name I am arraigned for desolating their provinces in India, I dare to reply that they are . . . the most flourishing of all the states in India. It was I who made them so. . . . I gave you all ; and you have rewarded me with confiscation, disgrace, and a life of impeachment."

From the beginning to the end of his trial he never failed to confront and contradict his accusers ; nor was Burke a whit more convinced of his atrocious villainy than was Hastings of his own spotless and unassailable innocence.

In February, 1792, Mr. Law [1] opened the defence. He began by remarking upon the disadvantages of those who had to meet the concentrated force, fire, and

[1] Afterwards Lord Ellenborough.

unbridled violence of the attack by a laborious, accurate, and tedious defence, by detecting fallacies, disentangling errors, and unveiling misrepresentations. He travelled over much ground that would now be scarcely thought worth traversing. It had been the theory of the prosecution that a golden age of peace and good government in India had preceded the intervention of the English in the affairs of that unfortunate country; and for the purpose of demolishing this hypothesis Law thought himself obliged to enter upon a general sketch of the history of Hindustan. He then proceeded to review the whole series of the transactions, from 1756 to 1786, with which Hastings had been in any way connected, in a speech which, although it intentionally gives things a turn favourable to his client, yet may be safely read as a clear and well-arranged historical summary, accurate on all salient points and material questions; and he vindicated the personal integrity of Hastings in terms which have never been refuted. Referring to the earlier days of Lord Clive, when the whole revenues of Bengal were virtually at the disposal of a few Englishmen, he said :

"At the time when so many millions, either in the shape of restitution for losses, of presents, or in other ways, were transferred from the country government to the English, to the amount, as stated, of more than £1,200,000, you do not find a single penny of all these sums ascribed or ascribable to Mr. Hastings. And it was upon that circumstance that the noble Lord (North), then in supreme trust of the British affairs, rested principally his recommendation of him, in full Parliament, for the situation of Governor-General. He stated him then as being the only flesh and blood which had resisted temptation in the infectious climate of India."

Law concluded with a very effective enumeration of
the successful acts of his government, with a description
of the indisputable prosperity and security in which
the Governor-General had left Bengal, with an appeal
to the strong expressions of sympathy that his prosecution had elicited from the natives of India, and with an
affirmation of his general ability and integrity. There
can be no doubt that this defence, as a close and cogent
argument sustained by a strong array of moderately-
stated facts, deserves attentive study by all who desire
to judge Hastings impartially; and the style of Law's
peroration might possibly be found as much to the taste
of the present age as the far more famous periods of
the orators who were against him. Plumer followed in
particular reply upon the question whether Hastings
was entitled to levy a fine on Cheyt Singh, which, as
he said, had been debated for ten years. Then came
the witnesses, and the Court rose after having sat
twenty-two days, beginning usually, as Hastings humbly
observed, at two in the afternoon and rising soon after
five.

In 1793 the trial was resumed with the reply on the
second charge, relating to the treatment of the Oude
Begums, when Law again took their Lordships through
the history of Hindustan from the establishment of
Mahommedanism in that country, to show that the
widows of Shuja-u-Dowlah had no right to detain the
treasures claimed by his successor. In this manner an
astounding mass of abstruse erudition, historical precedent, juridical texts, and oral testimony, drawn indiscriminately from Europe and Asia, was heaped and piled
up over every point, until the real issue and its true

aspect lay lost, hid, and shrivelled like a mummy under
a huge pyramid. The dreary and flat waste of the
voluminous record is studded here and there by these
monuments of useless labour set up over against each
other by the indefatigable energy of the disputants.
The Court itself produced a mournful and sepulchral
impression on the imagination of those who had seen
the commencement, and were still surveying the course,
of these slow-moving interminable proceedings ; the
attendance, sparse and attenuated, touched the mind
with a sense of mortality. Of one hundred and eighty-
six peers who had seen the Begum charge opened by
the prosecution, not more than twenty-eight, and usually
less, were now listening to the defence, and up to
October, 1793, one hundred and twenty-seven changes
had taken place in the peerage. Lord Thurlow in trying to upset Pitt had himself been upset, and had lost
the seals ; Lord Loughborough presided in his stead.
The defending counsel toiled on in the task of picking
to pieces the network of accusations, in dissecting pro-
positions and arguments, exposing different sides of the
same shield, setting one account of an affair against another
flatly opposed to it, proving that saints were sinners and
sinners saints, pouring cold water on the embers of the
smouldering invectives of Burke and Sheridan, until the
vast collection of contradictory proofs and arguments
must have become intellectually unmanageable. Burke
had described Nuncomar as a venerable priest, eminent
for his talents, of irreproachable morals, who never
appeared in public without exciting awe and exacting
respect. Dallas, on the other side, drew the portrait of
a " hoary intriguer," in whose aged breast fermented the

furious passions of youth, full of malice and turbulence, and perpetually planning the ruin of civil society. The managers had termed Muni Begum a common prostitute, who kept "the greatest gin-shop in all Asia"; the defence proved undeniably that she was a lady treated with every respect by all high officers, including Lord Cornwallis; and so on. The proceedings were varied in May by an indecorous attempt on the part of the Archbishop of York (Markham), whose son had been with Hastings at Benares, to interrupt Burke; and when a few days later the Court adjourned, the trial virtually closed with an address by Hastings on the termination of his defence:

"In the presence," he said, "of that Being from whom no secrets are hid, I do, upon a full review and scrutiny of my past life, unequivocally and conscientiously declare that in the administration of that trust of government which was so many years confided to me, I did in no instance intentionally sacrifice the interest of my country to any private views of personal advantage; that, according to my best skill and judgment I invariably promoted the essential interests of my employers, the happiness and prosperity of the people committed to my charge, and the welfare and honour of my country."

He protested before God that he had at no time possessed a fortune which at its utmost exceeded £100,000; that all his property stood pledged for defraying the cost of the trial; and that there, and there only, were "the enormous fruits of thirteen years of imputed rapacity and peculation, and more than thirty years of active and important service." In imploring their Lordships to pass immediate judgment, he ventured to remind them that "in the long period of another year I may be numbered

with those among my noble judges whom I have, with
sorrow, seen drop off from year to year, and in aggrava-
tion of the loss by their deaths, I may lose the judgment
of their survivors by my own." However, the trial,
after debate in both Houses, with some sharp recrimination as to responsibility for delay and much criticism
of the immense costs, was adjourned to the session of
1794.

The principal incident of this session was the examination of the Marquis Cornwallis, who had now returned
from his seven years' Governor-Generalship of India, and
had been summoned by Hastings for the defence. He
stated in reply to questions that during the whole of his
residence in India no personal complaint against his predecessor had been received, that Hastings was much
esteemed and respected by the natives in general and
had rendered very essential services to his country. The
managers continued to cross-examine witnesses for the
defence ; but the proceedings were still very frequently
arrested by disputes over the admission of evidence ; [1]
for Burke proposed to put in and comment upon six folio
volumes of printed proceedings and correspondence, in
proof that Hastings was the author of the Mahratta war.
Then came the replies of the prosecution, when the
leading managers again spoke at length ; until finally
Burke summed up the case against the prisoner in a
speech which lasted nine days, and in which he again

---

[1] *Question.* "What impression did the letting of the lands to
Kullian Singh make on the inhabitants of the country ? "
Answer. "They heard it with terror and dismay." After nearly
a whole day's argument, and reference to the judges, Law got this
answer expunged from the record.

lashed Hastings severely, and defended the use of strong words in describing his conduct. The language of the Commons of England, he said, was rustic but intelligible; they had not learnt the refinement of Indian corruption, and the application of fine and emollient terms to bad actions proved the degeneracy of the present age. Sir Edward Coke was wrong in calling Raleigh a spider of hell, but if he had given the appellation to Hastings, Coke would have erred more against decorum than truth. It must be admitted that the display of such ever-burning animosity and such constant use of figurative execration were unworthy of a great statesman and splendid orator, a man of lofty patriotism and political genius, kindly-hearted and beloved in private life. But he was suffering from public disgust and private anxieties; and the luminous energies of his mind had now been turned upon the scene, to which he alluded at the conclusion of his final address, of barbarities, disorders, and bloody proscriptions, amid which Church and State in France were subsiding into what seemed to him irreparable ruin. The epithets which he now so urgently needed for the Jacobins, for Danton and Robespierre, for regicides and brutal assassins of women, had lost some of their force by prodigal expenditure upon Hastings; and he had blunted the edge of his trenchant eloquence by hacking at his own countrymen. He ended his speech by declaring that the Commons awaited with trembling solicitude the issue of a cause on which they had been employed for twenty-two years, of which seven had been passed in this trial; he alluded to the destruction of the Parliament of Paris, a high court almost as dignified as that which he was then addressing; and he reminded

their Lordships that if their fate should be to pass also
under the guillotine, their last hours would be quieted
by the consciousness of having done justice in the great
cause now before them.

Here ended the business of the management, and a
vote of thanks to the managers, moved by Pitt, was
carried by a majority in the Commons, to the somewhat
unreasonable mortification of Hastings. Early in 1795
came the eighth and last session, when the Lords resolved
themselves into a committee of the whole House for the
consideration of the matter of the trial. Lord Thurlow
argued warmly in favour of Hastings ; while Lord
Loughborough, the Chancellor, was against him, until
after discussion for several days their Lordships adjourned
to give judgment in Westminster Hall, where Warren
Hastings was acquitted, in April, 1795, by a large
majority on each of the sixteen questions that were put
to the vote. Burke wrote in 1796 to Lord Loughborough,
who had voted Hastings guilty on thirteen out of the
sixteen counts :

" As to the acquittal, that it was total I was surprised at ;
that it should be so in a good measure I expected from the
incredible corruption of the time."

It should be understood that of the twenty articles of
impeachment originally presented at the bar of the House
of Lords, only six were regularly proceeded upon. The
trial, from the opening of the proceedings to the vote of
acquittal, extended over seven sessions of Parliament—
from February, 1788, to April, 1795—and occupied one
hundred and forty-eight sittings of the Court; though
the actual sittings in open Court to hear argument and
evidence are given in the Report of the Commons Com-

mittee at one hundred and eighteen.[1] The greatest
number of Lords that sat at any time upon the Court
was one hundred and sixty-eight; but in general there
were from thirty to fifty; and there had been in all
one hundred and eighty changes, from death or other
causes, during the proceedings. The expenses of the
accused had, by his own computation, amounted to about
£100,000, of which £75,000 were verified legal costs;
the expenses of the prosecution had also been very large.

[1] Distribution of sitting days—

			Days.
In the year 1788 the Court sat .	.	.	35
,,　　1789　　,,	.	.	17
,,　　1790　　,,	.	.	14
,,　　1791　　,,	.	.	5
,,　　1792　　,,	.	.	22
,,　　1793　　,,	.	.	22
,,　　1794 to March 1st .	.	.	3
			118

—*Report of Commons Committee.*

CHAPTER IX

LAST YEARS

IT has been thought expedient to give some particular account of this extraordinary trial, as being on the whole the most remarkable and perhaps the most generally interesting incident of the life of Hastings, and as illustrating the manners of the time, the temper of that generation of Englishmen before whom Hastings was arraigned, and the state of public opinion that is represented, not unfairly, by the verdict. Lord Campbell says that the interest in these proceedings had greatly declined, and that public sympathy was all with the accused, which is easily intelligible when we remember that the trial ended amid the rising uproar and conflagration of the French Revolution, and at the outbreak of one of the fiercest and longest wars in modern English history. At a moment when a day's journey to France could give the English people a nearer and clearer view of real horrors and atrocities, of judicial murders, massacres, violent unjustifiable invasions and usurpations, the rapacity of conquest, and the plundering of weak principalities, it was not to be expected that the national feeling would continue to be deeply stirred by narratives of what happened a dozen years back in India, of the oppressions of Bengal ryots, of heavy fines levied on

Begums and zemindars, of treaties twisted by equivocation, or even of a single Brahmin's unmerited death by a
formal judicial sentence.   To the Englishmen of 1794-95
the later stages of the trial must inevitably have seemed
tame and tedious; like a fine piece of historic tragedy,
well acted and set out with footlights and costumes, but
thinly attended toward the close because some genuine
bloodshed is found to be going on outside in the neighbouring streets.   No one will deny that those who first
instituted these proceedings acted upon motives and
with objects that were laudable and disinterested.   They
were men of the highest reputation and patriotic spirit,
who were solicitous for the honour of their nation and
for the integrity of its agents in distant countries, exposed to all the temptations of irresistible power, and of
wealth that lay easily within the grasp of a strong hand.
They felt a keen sympathy with weak princes and subject races; they were resolved that the flag of England
should not fly over plundered provinces, that English
arms should not uphold an Oriental despotism, and that
the authority of Parliament should be made coextensive
with the involuntary spread of its dominion.   The first
Act of Parliament to regulate Indian affairs was passed
at a time (1773) when some such interposition was
urgently needed; the second Act, eleven years later, was
equally necessary to improve the machinery of the Indian
government, and to establish a tighter control.   But the
intervening period had been one of unexampled difficulty
and confusion, when our Indian polity was as yet quite
unsettled, when the right principles of administration
were still very imperfectly worked out, when England
herself was under an incapable and corrupt rule, and

when the scramble of conquest and commerce in the
east and the west was still going on among the nations
of Europe. Our earlier forefathers held it a good answer
to account for a man's death that he was slain in chance
medley; and it must be allowed that when Hastings had
to hold his ground and keep his head in the Indian
scuffles he took such weapons as came handiest, and was
determined that others should want before he did. He
did things that were bold, hard, and unjustifiable according to the standard of English proof, which ought always
to be the measure of Englishmen who represent their
country abroad. To hold a grand national inquisition
into his conduct, upon his return, was an intelligible and
not unreasonable proceeding; and the trial had several
beneficial results. It cleared off a cloud of misconcep-
tions, calumnies, exaggerations, and false notions generally
on both sides; it fixed and promulgated the standard
which the English people would in future insist upon
maintaining in their Indian administration; it bound
down the East India Company to better behaviour; it
served as an example and as a salutary warning, and it
relieved the national conscience. But the attempt to
make Hastings a sacrifice and a burnt-offering for the
sins of the people; the process of loading him with curses
and driving him away into the wilderness; of stoning
him with every epithet and metaphor that the English
language could supply for heaping ignominy on his head;
of keeping him seven years under an impeachment that
menaced him with ruin and infamy—these were blots
upon the prosecution and wide aberrations from the
true course of justice which disfigured the aspect of the
trial, distorted its aim, and had much to do with bringing

it to the lame and impotent conclusion [1] that Burke so bitterly denounced.

For the excessive duration of the proceedings the managers, who had many motives for expedition, do not seem to have been responsible. In 1794 a Committee of the Commons, appointed to inquire into the length of the trial, laid the whole blame on the Lords; whereupon Thurlow indignantly pronounced their report to be a scurrilous pamphlet, indecent and disgraceful, such as ought not to pass unpunished. The truth is that the procedure by Parliamentary impeachment, which had been generally used as a sharp popular remedy for the offences of great men, was plainly unsuited to a case that went upon a large collection of documentary evidence, and afforded scope for dissertations on politics and history, arguments over Asiatic customs and creeds, and dialectics upon the philosophy of geographical morals. The fact that the prosecution was managed by Parliamentary orators and the defence by eminent lawyers, clearly led to a conflict of ideas as to the rules and principles to be mutually observed, and materially impeded a precise fixing of the real issues upon which the interests of India and England certainly demanded an authoritative judgment. The custom of the age still permitted Chancellors and Secretaries of State to accuse each other of heinous political crimes; and the chiefs of parties abused each other like Homeric heroes. All this was tolerable in open warfare, and it partially explains the violence of the language used against Hastings; but it

[1] "To the perpetual infamy of a body which, God knows, I wish to be held in perpetual honour, I mean the House of Lords."—Burke to Lord Loughborough, January, 1795.

gave a very damaging tone of passion and prejudice to the prosecutors of a man who was precluded from replying upon equal terms.[1]

The final verdict was approved by and expressed the sense of the country. If Hastings had done wrong and deserved public censure rather than public honours, he had now suffered heavily ; and the single fact that his character for personal integrity, though vehemently attacked, had passed unscathed through strong temptations and such an ordeal as this trial, must have told powerfully upon a generation with whom incorruptibility was as yet, in common belief, something of a rare quality among politicians. The benefit of the acquittal did not go wholly to the score of the accused. Its effect was to confirm and ratify certain important acts of State for which he had been impeached ; and from which, be it remembered, the East India Company and the British nation derived large profits and political advantages. If Hastings, like Julius Cæsar, had been hard on subject princes, at any rate their ransoms did, as Mark Antony said, fill the public coffers. The prosecution had often been reminded, not very seriously or forcibly, that if their charges were established the reinstatement of Cheyt Singh in the Benares estate, the repayment of great sums of money to the Begums and the Nawab of Oude,

---

[1] " The impeachment of Warren Hastings is, I think, a blot on the judicial history of the country. It was monstrous that a man should be tortured at irregular intervals for seven years in order that a singularly incompetent tribunal might be addressed before an excited audience by Burke and Sheridan, in language far removed from the calmness with which an advocate for the prosecution ought to address a criminal court."—*History of Criminal Law*, by Sir James Stephen, i. 160.

and various other inconvenient measures of reparation, ought logically to follow. It is not probable that in any event this would have been thought necessary; for the Ministers might have adopted Sir John Falstaff's view in respect to the Gadshill subsidy, that paying back is double labour; but it had been proved that the Company benefited to the amount of several millions sterling by the transactions in Oude and Benares; and the result of the trial was to set at rest all questions of reopening these arrangements.

Immediately after his acquittal Hastings sent to the Chancellor of the Exchequer, Mr. Pitt, a petition praying that the House of Commons would indemnify him for his legal expenses. Pitt replied, as might have been expected, by a brief and formal refusal; while Burke protested to the Lord Chancellor against the infamy of condemning the Commons in costs and damages, and granting pensions to "the accused and the accursed." The matter was next brought before the Court of Proprietors, who voted him compensation and a pension out of the Indian revenues, after obtaining from him a full account of his debts and assets which proved his liabilities for costs of the trial to be very nearly equal to all his available resources; but the Board of Control decided against the legality of such an appropriation. And the matter was finally arranged by a compromise between the Government and the Company whereby Hastings received a pension of £4000 for twenty-eight and a half years, with a large payment in advance and a loan of £50,000 free of interest. But he had been laying out £60,000 on the purchase of the Daylesford estate, and another £60,000 were still due for law charges. The

failure of a "great Dutch house in the city" had swept
away a considerable sum deposited there by Mrs. Hastings.   Dr. French Lawrence wrote to Burke in 1797 a
hilarious letter upon this piece of news; and Burke
replies with sombre satisfaction, saying also that the
grants of public money to Hastings amounted to a condemnation of himself as the persecutor of innocence and
merit.   In another letter to Lawrence he remarks, "they
are nursing up Hastings for the peerage," and asks
whether he (Burke) is to be called in to prove how right
it is "to raise a sharping bullock contractor above the
common level of citizens."   Such was the inextinguish-
able ire of that celestial mind; but Burke was now very
soon to be laid where his heart could no more be lacerated
by disappointment and savage indignation.   Hastings
survived him twenty years; the peerage never came,
and notwithstanding advances, loans, and mortgages
on his pension and his lands, he was for some years
afterward in pecuniary straits, until in 1804 a fresh interposition of the authorities placed his income on a very
moderate but secure footing.

Thenceforward Hastings passed many years at Daylesford, living a life of retirement and comparative obscurity
after the manner of those who settled down in an outlying English county at the beginning of this century,
when men rarely took to a fresh occupation after middle
age, and when a seat in Parliament offered almost the
only serious employment beyond rural pursuits to an
active country gentleman.   He had not the modern
resource of contributing to literary reviews, or of joining
archæological societies or city companies; he farmed,
rode, read and admired Scott, and wrote verses in the

style of the period. The incidents which varied the even
tenor of such an existence were few and of little moment.
In 1804 Mr. Addington, baited by the Opposition, ill-
supported by some of his friends, and depressed by the
feeling that the nation at large preferred Pitt to him as
chief minister at a crisis when Bonaparte threatened an
invasion of England, was about to resign. Hastings,
who had been under some obligation to Addington for
sympathy and assistance, asked and obtained an audience
for the purpose of dissuading him. The interview,
which Macaulay treats scornfully, is described by Gleig
with unction and respectful deference to "the pure-
minded and venerable statesman" whom Hastings
addressed with a formal remonstrance against yielding
to pressure. He assured Addington that the voice of
the House of Commons was not the voice of the people ;
that during the course of the last week he had scarcely
seen man or woman who did not execrate the confederacy
(of Pitt, Fox, and the Grenvilles) that had been formed
against the Minister ; that, on the contrary, they were
exceedingly well satisfied with the administration, and
that even his enemies admitted Addington's integrity
while they profligately sneered at it. The language is
courageous, but there is in it an echo of his own past
injuries and resentments ; particularly when he goes on
to make light of the Minister's deficiency in oratory—
"that waste of words and time which is the invariable
substitute for useful matter and progressive action"; and
the tone leaves on the reader, as it probably did on
Addington, an impression that Hastings had by no
means mastered the art or learnt the ways of English
politics. He could hardly have failed to see that

Pitt's popularity, parliamentary influence, and governing capacity made him a far better leader of the nation at the climax of a great struggle than Addington; but he was probably actuated by a certain degree of animosity toward Pitt and Fox, who were about to coalesce; and it had never been his own habit to resign when he was abused, attacked, and overmatched. Nor must it be forgotten that Fox himself was of opinion at the time that Addington need not have resigned while he had a majority in the House. Hastings did not succeed in convincing Addington; but on the contrary Addington convinced Hastings, who went away satisfied that the Minister's only course was to resign, and possibly thinking that he himself would have tried a very different line of conduct if he could only have had Addington's chance of commanding the national ship in a storm. Soon afterward came the political ruin of Lord Melville, who just escaped impeachment for corruption, to the great distress and in some degree to the discredit of Pitt. In his correspondence Hastings refers to this event without bitterness; yet he may have thought that there was some retribution in the fate of Dundas, who had taken a large though indirect share in the promotion of similar imputations against him.

When the death of Pitt in January, 1806, dissolved the Tory Ministry, Hastings, like his enemy Francis, seems to have thought that the accession to office of Lord Grenville and the Whigs might afford him a chance of returning to active employ, and that some members of the Cabinet might be inclined to look favourably on his claims. That both Francis and Hastings should have applied almost simultaneously (in the spring of 1806) to

the Regent and the new Ministers for public office and
personal distinction, is at least a coincidence and a
curious reappearance of their ancient rivalry, for each
of the two men must have been heartily sure that the
other deserved nothing but dishonour and chastisement.
They may at any rate have been consoled by each other's
failure; although their overtures were made in a very
different style and temper.   Both of them had in mind
the Governor-Generalship of India.   Francis wanted to
succeed Lord Cornwallis, and quarrelled viciously with
Fox and Lord Grenville because they refused to appoint
him; his intrigues at Court were equally unsuccessful,
and all he got was a Civil Knight Companionship of the
Bath.   Hastings merely obtained audience of the Prince
of Wales, when after modestly saying that he had now
relinquished his thoughts of public office, he suggested
that the House of Commons might make him some
reparation for the injuries that he had suffered, and also
expressed a desire for some title in which his wife, " the
best and most amiable of women," might participate.
The Prince professed much regard for him, and appears
to have endeavoured to further his wishes; but the
Cabinet were unwilling to give their assent, because
any public recognition of his merits might imply a
condemnation of the measures formerly taken against
him by some of the Ministers.   That this was their
attitude toward him Hastings gathered from an interview
with Lord Moira on the subject; and although some
hope was held out that the Prince's influence might
nevertheless prevail, he seems to have drawn back at
once.   " I never," he said to Lord Moira, " will receive
a favour without an acknowledgment; much less will

I accept a favour from men who have done me great
personal wrongs, though the act so construed should
be the result of their submission to a different consideration."

From that time forward he withdrew almost entirely
from connexion with public affairs; nor does his correspondence show many references even to India, where
the position of the English Government had changed
rapidly and radically since he left the country. The
transformation of the chief governorship of a chartered
commercial company into a senatorial proconsulship had
been completed; the first two parliamentary Governors-
General, Cornwallis and Wellesley, had made good use
of their time; the strength of the great native powers
against whom Hastings had so painfully contended was
effectually broken; and on their ruins a vast territorial
sovereignty had been established. In 1786 Hastings
had been impeached (among other matters) for having
taken from the Mahrattas the little island of Salsette, on
on which now stands a part of the town of Bombay.
In 1806 the Mahratta confederacy had lost, by war, whole
provinces extending into the heart of India: the dynasty
of Hyder Ali had disappeared from Mysore; and half
the possessions of the Oude ruler had been transferred
to the British. How much the nature of a Governor-
General's business, and his method of conducting it, had
altered since the days of Hastings, may be inferred from
a passage in one of his letters, where he regrets the
absence of Lord Minto (an ancient enemy of the impeachment period) from Calcutta, "as it must be productive
of all the evils of an insufficient and unresponsible
government."

"I am not afraid of saying that no future Governor-General will discharge his duty properly that does not do as I did—inspect the weekly or monthly details of every department, and give his instructions as often to the head of it. This duty he can only perform by being constantly on the spot; it cannot be done by delegation."

To those who know the magnitude and multiplicity of the affairs which now fill up a Governor-General's time, this conception of his duty will seem rather obsolete; and indeed it was out of date in 1806, when Hastings wrote. In fact the changes, political and administrative, that took place in India between 1786 and 1806 almost equalled those which Europe underwent during the same period; nor was any such great stride forward made again for over forty years, until the Punjab had been subdued, and the territories of two dynasties with whom Hastings had been very closely connected, the Nawabs of Oude and the Bhonsla Rajahs of Nagpore, were finally incorporated with the British empire.

In 1813, when the revision of the Company's charter came before Parliament, Hastings was summoned by both Houses to give evidence. The brief and probably inaccurate report of his examination by the Committee of the Commons is to some extent disappointing. The tendency of his views is very strongly conservative—it might be called, even then, old-fashioned; but he had been nearly thirty years absent from India, and the effect of time in spoiling the soundest experience and the most valuable opinions is distinctly perceptible. It is indeed remarkable that while people are constantly describing India as of all countries the most conservative and the slowest to change, yet no political knowledge falls more rapidly out of date or grows musty sooner

than that which is brought back from India; the funda-
mental principles being always excepted. He was
treated, as is well known, with particular respect.

" By the Commons I was under examination between
three and four hours, and when I was ordered to withdraw,
and was retiring, all the members by one simultaneous im-
pulse rose with their heads uncovered, and stood in silence
till I passed the door of their chamber. The House was
unusually crowded. The same honour was paid to me,
though of course with a more direct intention, by the Lords."

Two or three months later the University of Oxford
conferred on him the honorary degree of Doctor of Law,
when his reception in the theatre was very flattering;
he was much pleased by Dr. Phillimore's elegant Latin
oration, and still more by a sonorous poem which Sir
Elijah Impey indited upon the occasion. In 1814 his
name was added to the list of Privy Councillors—an
honour that Mr. Gleig seems inclined most unnecessarily
to attribute to the stimulative effect upon the good feelings of the nation at large produced by the joy and
excitement at the ending of the long French war, and to
"the operation of this common principle of human
nature in the highest quarter," to wit, the Prince Regent.
The Prince presented him to the allied sovereigns, "as
the most deserving and at the same time one of the
worst used men in the empire"; and he promised still
greater distinctions, but no performance followed; and
Hastings returned finally to country life at Daylesford,
varied by occasional visits to London. He had presided
at a dinner given by Anglo-Indian gentlemen to the
Duke of Wellington; but he was a little troubled at the
newspaper having said, in reporting his speech, that his

voice was feeble. At Daylesford he busied himself
with superintending the work of restoring his parish
church; making the remark, evidently derived from
Indian recollections, that an occupation which engages
the attention upon visible and palpable objects is most
suited to infirm and simple minds, just as idols are
necessary to worship in certain stages. His health
was not seriously impaired up to the spring of 1818,
when the infirmities of old age closed in upon him,
and he became gradually worse until after an illness
of six weeks he died on August 18th, 1818. About
a fortnight before his death he dictated a letter conveying (through a friend) to the Court of Directors
his earnest desire for the continuance of his annuity to
his wife, "the dearest object of all my mortal concerns,"
to whom, he said, it was due that he had been able to
maintain the affairs of the Company for thirteen years
in vigour, respect, and credit; and whose independent
fortitude and presence of mind had on one occasion
been the means of guarding a province of their dominion
from impending ruin. Mrs. Hastings survived him
some years, and was over ninety years of age when she
died; but it is not wonderful that the application failed
entirely, remembering that even Lord Nelson's last testa-
mentary appeal on behalf of a woman ("the only favour
I ask of my king and my country at this moment when
I am going to fight their battle") had been rejected and
utterly disregarded.

Such battles as Hastings waged had been long
finished, and were comparatively inglorious. He lies
buried in a vault of Daylesford Church; and in Westminster Abbey a bust and an inscription commemorate

the name and career of a man who, rising early to high
place and power, held an office of the greatest importance to his country for thirteen years by sheer force of
character and tenaciousness against adversity ; and who
spent the next seven years in defending himself before
a nation which accepted the benefits but disliked the
ways of his too masterly activity. He was a man of
great original capacity, whose special qualities, and
their defects, had been exercised and drawn out by a
course of very practical training. He owed nothing to
the study of text-books, nothing to accepted usage,
official precedent, professional tradition, or even to the
pressure of public opinion which limits and shapes the
possibilities of statesmanship. He had been shipped
out to India a raw lad, and had there been left to gather
his experience among the extraordinary incidents of
Anglo-Indian politics in their earliest, roughest, and most
rudimentary stage. He had to work with a set of adventurous and rather unscrupulous Englishmen in dealing
with a subject population of a totally different nature ;
he found himself in a situation of much hazard, where
most things were permissible and very few things impossible, where written laws were unknown, where the
common law and conventions of civilised States were as
yet unrecognised, and where the primitive necessity of
self-preservation, which lies at the basis of the most
firmly organised societies, stood constantly and markedly
in the foreground. There is no such school for practical
politics as Asia, where the good old rules of taking and
keeping still prevail side by side with the most solemn
and laudable precepts of justice and virtue ; and where
inconsistencies between acts and axioms trouble no one.

It was this training that strengthened the natural aptitude of Hastings for fertility of resource, firmness of
temper, self-reliance, patience, equanimity, and reserve,
which served him well at critical moments and enabled
him to outlast protracted opposition.   But it also
enhanced his love of power, his autocratic disposition,
and his inability to see or admit that a view may have
been wrong, or an action blameworthy.   His unrivalled
grasp of detail, his thorough knowledge of the needs and
capabilities of Bengal, gave full scope to his talent for
administrative organisation ; while in the general range
of his tastes and interests he seems to have gone far
beyond his Anglo-Indian contemporaries.   The very remarkable journey of Mr. Bogle to the court of the Teshoo
Lama in Tibet was made entirely under the initiative and
encouragement of Hastings ; and while he was always
ready to promote geographical exploration he was still
more active in advancing schemes for education and the
revival of Oriental learning.   The Mahommedan college
which he instituted in Calcutta still flourishes : Sir
William Jones acknowledged the support he gave to the
Asiatic Society ; and the great interest he took in the
translation and digest of Hindu laws suggested to
Burke various ironical reflections on his supposed disregard of them.

Looking back on the character and career of Hastings,
we may say that he possessed some of the strongest
inbred qualities and defects of an Englishman, developed
and directed by very remarkable circumstances.   He
showed a genius for pioneering administration that would
have won him distinction at any epoch of our Indian

history.   His fortune brought him forward in the transitional period between Clive and Cornwallis, when the confusion of new conquest was still fermenting, and when the methods of irregular, unrecognised rulership had been discountenanced but not discontinued ; when the conscience of the nation demanded orderly government before it had become altogether practicable.   It is no wonder that among the sundry and manifold difficulties of such a period, a man of his training and temper should have occasionally done things that are hard to justify and easy to condemn, or that his public acts should have brought him to the verge of private ruin.   For he was undoubtedly cast in the type, so constantly recurrent in political history, of the sons of Zeruiah, and he very nearly earned their historical reward.

THE END